MW00638135

MAKING AND FULFILLING YOUR DREAMS AS A LEADER

A PRACTICAL GUIDE FOR FORMULATING AND EXECUTING STRATEGY

SECOND EDITION

CARL WELTE

ISBN: 978-1-957203-17-1 (sc)
ISBN: 978-1-957203-18-8 (hc)
ISBN: 978-1-957203-19-5 (e)

Because of the dynamic nature of the Internet, any web addresses or
links contained in this book may have changed since publication and
may no longer be valid. The views expressed in this work are solely those
of the author and do not necessarily reflect the views of the publisher,
and the publisher hereby disclaims any responsibility for them.

THE EWINGS PUBLISHING

The Ewings Publishing LLC
One Galleria Blvd., Suite 1900, Metairie, LA 70001
1-888-421-2397

*To all leaders who with wisdom and perseverance strive
to make positive changes for the common good.*

CONTENTS

PREFACE TO THE SECOND EDITION

This new and improved edition of *Making and Fulfilling Your Dreams as a Leader* incorporates the increased wisdom and knowledge I have gained regarding strategy formulation and execution since the initial version was published in 2014. The increased knowledge was gained through my ongoing study of effective organizations and leaders, and the continuing use of the Strategic Framework with clients.

Enhancements have been made throughout the book to provide greater clarity relative to the Strategic Framework and the supporting concepts, structures, processes, and tools.

The only change to the Strategic Framework model itself is the addition of a Big Dream Vision at the onset of the envisioning process. I have come to realize and appreciate the importance of a big dream or ultimate quest. A big dream better equips the organization to craft powerful and compelling interim visions in moving forward. It also helps answer, along with the organization's purpose, the important WHY question for the organization. WHY do we exist? And, what is our ultimate quest?

I have added several appendices to help leaders apply the various aspects of the Strategic Framework. There is also a self-coaching appendix for any personal development needs the leader may care to work on.

ACKNOWLEDGMENTS

I am grateful to the many organizations for which I have worked as a leader or consultant and the challenging opportunities they have afforded me to learn and grow and acquire my knowledge of leadership and organizational effectiveness. I am also grateful to the wonderful people who have provided me valuable learning experiences, mentoring, and coaching along the way.

One of the things I have always cherished about leadership and organizational consulting is that each engagement is unique, allowing for growth and adding greater value to my clients.

INTRODUCTION

....

Leaders are dreamers…idealists…possibility thinkers. All enterprises, big or small, begin with the belief that what's merely an image today can one day be made real. It's this belief that sustains leaders through the difficult times.

—Kouzes and Posner, *The Leadership Challenge*

There are two imperatives for assuring sustained organization success.

The first imperative is a *sound strategy*. A strategy that clearly articulates the organization's identity, direction, and plans for achieving the sound strategy.

The second imperative is *a work culture that fosters genuine commitment*. A committed workforce is one where people "want to perform" rather than feeling that they "have to perform", which is compliance. A committed workforce is one in which people want to work together to struggle to achieve shared aspirations. That is right, struggle. A committed workforce realizes that anything worth striving for does not come easy. They are motivated to do whatever it takes to work toward achieving important shared aspirations.

My book, *Building Commitment; A Leader's Guide to Unleashing the Human Potential at Work*[1], addresses the second imperative. It provides the leader with practical and proven concepts, structures, processes, practices and tools for building and maintaining a work culture that fosters commitment. It is a natural follow on to *Making and Fulfilling Your Dreams as a Leader.*

This book addresses the first imperative. Its purpose is to enable you as a leader–regardless of business sector or organizational level –to formulate and execute a sound strategy. The book equips you with a strategic framework to use on an ongoing basis to establish and live your organizational identity and struggle to achieve your direction in addressing important current and emerging realities.

Based on their years of ongoing global research and application of their *Leadership Practices Inventory*, a leadership assessment instrument that complements their *The Leadership Challenge* book and workshops, James Kouzes and Barry Posner have identified formulating and executing a sound strategy as being by far the number one challenge for most leaders. And an area in which most leaders are not very good at and are reluctant to tackle. Yet it is so vital. It is the leader's job number one. The intent of this book is to equip you with the clarity, confidence, and competence to take on this challenge and be successful in doing so.

The book guides you through each phase of formulating and executing a sound strategy to enable you to take your personal journey in making and fulfilling your dreams as a leader.

The need for focus and effective execution is more important today than ever in our increasingly, fast paced, changing world. Opportunities and challenges abound. But leaders and their organizations need to be ready to make such opportunities work for them. The book equips you as leader to engage in the requisite quality thinking and interacting to help create the future and to propel your organization forward. The book guides you through the entire strategy formulation and execution cycle. Each chapter however stands on its own.

The first chapter sets the stage for the book by underscoring the importance of effective leadership and having shared aspirations necessary for organizational success. The Strategic Framework Model is used throughout the book to guide you through the cycle. Leadership behaviors critical for working with your leadership team in developing a sound strategy are also discussed in this initial chapter.

The book then proceeds chapter by chapter to walk you through the various dimensions and components of the Strategic Framework Model and give you the requisite knowledge and practical and proven methodologies to be a strategic leader.

Part I, "Formulating Strategy: Identity" focuses on defining the organizations DNA. That is, its core ideologies. "Who we are" and "What we stand for". The first two chapters in this section walk you through the two components of the Identity dimension: defining Purpose and clarifying Core Values. The third chapter is aimed at helping you identify and define any unique capabilities that may add to your articulating your organizational identity.

Part II, "Formulating Strategy: Direction", focuses on creating the future. The first chapter in this section, chapter 5, speaks to articulating a Big Dream Vision that serves as a constant focal point for all efforts in moving forward. A North Star.

Chapter 6, shows you how to conduct a Situation Analysis to identify and prioritize current and emerging opportunities and challenges that need to be addressed in moving forward toward your Big Dream Vision. The Situation Analysis helps your leadership team identify relevant trends, gain important insights and assess your organizational capability to get you all on the same page.

The result of your analysis allows you to logically craft a Translatable Interim Vision as detailed in chapter 7. An interim vision that is specific enough for you to develop a Strategic Path, the subject of chapter 8. Chapter 9 shows you how to craft viable action plans to allow you to achieve your various strategies.

Part III, "Executing Strategy", speaks to, in chapter 10, the essential leadership behaviors needed for implementing your sound strategy. This chapter also provides some useful structural mechanisms for effectively executing your strategy.

The intent is that this book will serve as a valuable resource to you on an ongoing basis for building and sustaining a sound strategy for your organization and in so doing fulfilling your dreams.

SHARED ASPIRATIONS:
A LEADERSHIP IMPERATIVE

Leaders get people moving. They energize and mobilize. They take people and organizations to places they have never been before.

–Jim Kouzes and Barry Posner,
The Leadership Challenge

The work of the organization consists of three broad categories: technical work, management work, and leadership.

Figure 1.1 The Work of the Organization

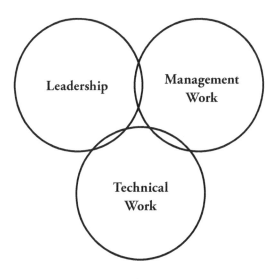

Technical Work   The direct application of physical and mental effort to provide the organization's products or services.

Management Work   The coordination of diverse activities to achieve desired results. The focus of management work is the here and now.

Leadership   The art of mobilizing others to want to struggle for shared aspirations.[1] The focus of leadership is the future.

All three categories of organizational work are critical. The importance of technical work, directly producing the organization's products and services is obvious. But without coordination provided by effective management confusion and inefficiencies abound. And without effective leadership the organization becomes mired in the status quo, or perhaps backslides. The status quo is not an option, especially in today's fast-paced world.

Relating to leadership and management work there is a phenomenon that every leader and manager needs to be keenly aware of and manage accordingly. We can call it the *Principle of Technical Priority*. This important principle posits that given a choice most managers would rather do technical work over management work. And for obvious reasons related to human nature. Technical work as compared to management work is most times more tangible, more action-oriented, and provides for more immediate and specific performance feedback. In addition, most managers feel more competent performing technical work, at least initially. This is especially true of the manager who has never managed before. And there is also the fear that one will become technically obsolete unless the technical know-how and skills are continually updated and honed. And in many instances the individual was selected for the managerial position based primarily on their technical acumen.

The result of the technical priority principle going unchecked is that a significant management gap can occur between the appropriate amount of management work being performed and the amount that should be performed throughout the organization, in any particular organizational unit, or by a specific manager. And we are just talking quantity here, not quality.

So, what needs to happen to prevent such a management gap from occurring? The answer is that the organization and its supervising managers need to make it matter for managers to manage. Managers need to be held accountable for performing the correct balance of management work in their respective positions in addition to their technical work. And to manage effectively.

Managers need to be properly trained, receive ongoing performance coaching and constructive feedback, and be provided challenging experiences to allow for continuing management learning and growth. And the organization's recognition and rewards systems need to reinforce the desired performance.

Given the proper direction and guidance as delineated above, there is no reason that most people who have the capabilities to perform the managerial responsibilities of the position for which they were selected should not succeed and continually learn and grow.

* * *

The focus of this book is leadership. Specifically formulating and executing a sound strategy consisting of shared aspirations to take the organization to where it needs and wants to go. So, let's talk more specifically about the relationship between leadership and this book.

3

Based on their extensive global research spanning three decades James Kouzes and Barry Posner, as detailed in their best-selling book *The Leadership Challenge*[2], have identified "the five practices of exemplary leaders". These practices are:

1. Model the Way
2. Inspire a Shared Vision
3. Challenge the Process
4. Enable others to Act
5. Encourage the Heart

These five practices and the two objectives for each practice, along with the six behaviors for each practice that constitute their *Leadership Practices Inventory* assessment instrument have withstood the test of time and proven to be valid in all cultures globally, in all business sectors, and at all levels of the organization.

Making and Fulfilling Your Dreams as a Leader provides you with practical and proven methods to successfully apply all of these practices, especially the first three: Model the Way; Inspire a Shared Vision; and, Challenge the Process. Effectively applying these first three practices is essential if you as a leader are going to create shared aspirations and mobilize and energize people to want to strive to live and achieve such aspirations.

To further make the point for the critical nature of shared aspirations we turn to the seminal work of Jim Collins and Jerry Porras captured in their book *Built to Last*.[3]

In their research the authors looked at what makes the truly successful companies outperform other companies in their respective industries. Their research destroyed the commonly held belief that only charismatic, visionary leaders can build visionary companies. What they discovered is that the exceptional companies were passionate about *both* defining and preserving their core ideologies (the "Identity" dimension in this book) and stimulating progress in their relevant external environment or marketplace (the "Direction" dimension in this book). A well-crafted identity and direction constitute the sound strategy talked about in this book.

The Strategic Framework model shown in Figure 1.2 consists of both an identity and direction dimension. These two dimensions and their related components are the strategy formulation part of the model. The third dimension focuses on working the strategy, the strategy execution part of the model.

This model is the core of the book. The succeeding chapters take you step by step through the dimensions and the related components of the model to allow you to engage in quality thinking and interacting to develop and implement your sound strategy.

Figure 1.2 Strategic Framework

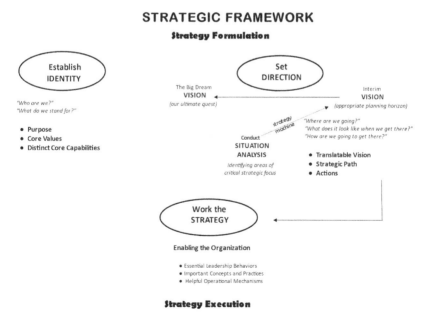

5

The identity dimension defines the organization's core ideologies. Why it exists. It's purpose. And what it stands for. It's core values. An organization's identity is the foundation upon which it is built. Once properly defined it is relatively timeless.

The direction dimension on the other hand needs to change as the organization envisions its ideal future, its big dream and resultant translatable interim vision or visions, and the evolving strategies, the strategic path, and resultant actions to make it happen.

The purpose of the direction dimension is to allow the organization to stimulate progress in its relevant external environment or marketplace in pursuit of its big dream. To do so the organization needs to continually engage in strategic thinking and planning "from the outside in" so it can best influence, adapt to, and align with its unique external context. Strategic thinking and planning by starting with what is happening externally also protects the organization in getting caught up in their own mental models and perhaps success and assuming what has worked in the past will also work in the future. It avoids myopic and insular leadership thinking. For staff departments within an organization their relevant external environment most often is the line departments they serve in the organization.

The purpose of a situation analysis is to conduct a scan of the organization's relevant external and internal environments to identify critical areas of strategic focus. Such analysis needs to be conducted periodically to allow the organization to identify and address current and emerging trends, opportunities, and challenges.

Even if it does a good job of formulating strategy, a large majority of organizations fall short in executing the strategy. Living and working the strategy on an ongoing basis has to be priority number one for the organization's leadership. Leaders need to model the way and be purposeful regarding their behavior. They need to make use of helpful mechanisms to help work the strategy and achieve desired results.

The Strategic Framework serves as a valuable model for leaders in all realms and levels of the organization. The rigor in which it is applied may understandably be less as strategy formulation cascades down through the organization. Regardless, organizational units need to interpret, align, and contribute to the overall strategic intent received from above. At a minimum local leaders should have for their respective units a well thought out purpose, a dream, and a set of relevant evolving strategies to move forward and make significant contributions.

Leader Behavior in Developing Shared Aspirations

Developing shared aspirations begins with you, the leader, and your leadership team. You need to interact with your leadership team in a genuine and qualitative manner throughout the entire process of formulating and executing your sound strategy. This does not mean however that your behavior will be or should be highly participative. For true leadership starts from within the leader. You need to believe in what you are doing. Developing a sound strategy does not require an all-out democratic process. This is especially true when it comes to clarifying values.

To be an effective leader, whether it comes to developing a sound strategy or in general, you need to vary your behavior to fit the situation. At times you should be highly directive. At other times the situation may call for a highly participative approach. On other occasions delegating decision making with clear expectations may be in order.

In choosing the appropriate leader behavior you need to assess the various situational variables at play. The most critical of these variables are the importance of the decision, its acceptance, and who has the requisite knowledge and experience for making a quality decision and implementing it.

In most cases you will want to engage your leadership team in quality thinking and interacting in part or throughout formulating your sound strategy, and certainly in executing it. Meaningful involvement will most likely improve the quality of strategy formulation and will certainly increase its acceptance and buy-in. People tend to own things they help create.

The model below identifies the various decision-making options available to you as a leader.

Figure 1.3 Leader Decision-Making Options

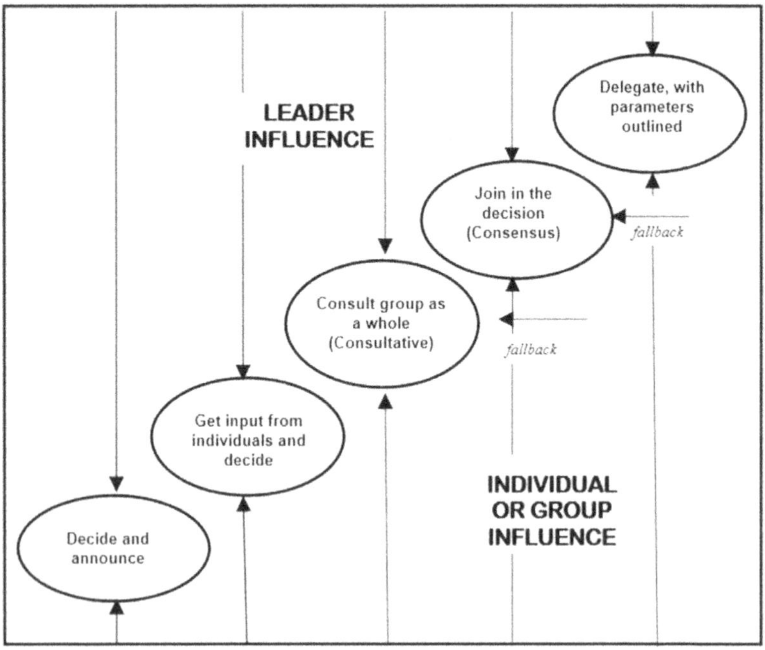

An important point for you to realize as a leader is that as you plow new ground not everyone is going to be with you. Consequently, you need to develop an "edge". That is, you need the courage to see reality and act on it. To make the tough decisions even though they may not be popular.[4]

A corollary is that sometimes people may not share your zeal about the decision of the course of action because they may not have had the same time to ponder it as you have. Or they do not fully appreciate all the considerations that went into the decision making. In such cases, hopefully the acceptance of the decision will increase as they experience the results. But then, it may not. Again, this is where you need to exhibit your edge or courage as a leader.

Once you as the leader have completed the required quality thinking and interacting with your leadership team in formulating the organizational sound strategy you then need to engage the organization as a whole, or the impacted segments of the organization, to allow people to understand and support the strategy. In other words, build shared aspirations.

What you do not want to do is what many organizations do. That is to just "roll it out". Rollouts do not work. You need to put in the necessary quality time and effort to help the people understand and support the strategy. And this may take time.

I

FORMULATING STRATEGY: IDENTITY

The identity dimension of formulating strategy focuses on why the organization exists (Purpose) and what it stands for (Core Values). These two components of identity describe the organization's core ideologies and provide a foundation from which to create the future and move forward.

Identity allows you to stay on course and not wander off and become distracted in pursuit of opportunities that on the surface seem appealing but do not really align or support what you are all about.

Chapter 2 shows you how to craft a powerful purpose. Chapter 3 shows you how to clarify a set of core values to serve as an everyday guide for you and your organization's everyday thinking and behavior.

Chapter 4 discusses an organization's distinct core capabilities, if indeed any exist. Such capabilities, if any exist, are not directly a part of purpose or core values. But they can be helpful in identifying and defining purpose and core values. Such capabilities can also be useful in developing direction in moving forward.

2

DEFINING PURPOSE: WHY DO WE EXIST?

An organization's purpose would seem to be obvious…
but rarely is.

—Peter Drucker

Start with WHY.

—Simon Sinek

"Why do we exist?"
"What do we stand for?"
⟶ • Purpose
• Core Values

What Is Purpose?

Purpose   The fundamental reason an organization or organizational unit
exists.

Purpose answers the questions:
Why do we exist?
What is our business? What should it be?

13

As stated by Peter Drucker above, an organization's purpose would seem to be quite straightforward. A steel mill makes steel; an insurance company underwrites risks; and a bank lends money. But, "What is our business?" is almost always a difficult question to answer. And the right answer is usually not obvious.[1]

Drucker emphasizes specifically answering "What is our business?" is the first responsibility of top management, be it the organization as a whole or an organizational unit. He stresses that this critical question rarely gets the reflective thinking it deserves. The question often sparks dissent because there is never one right answer. This inadequate attention to purpose, Drucker argues, is the single most important cause of business frustration and failure.[2]

Purpose is timeless. It serves, along with core values, as the foundation for the organization. The launching pad from which to create its future.

However, as an organization experiences stages in its life cycle it may need to rethink its purpose to stay viable. Figure 2.1 depicts the typical stages of evolution an organization goes through over time if indeed it continues to exist.

Figure 2.1 The Evolution of a Business or Organization

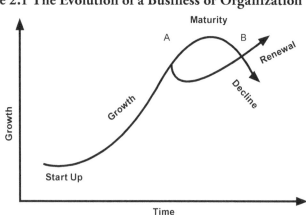

The speed with which an organization may experience these various stages, if indeed it does, is influenced by such factors as the dynamic nature of the industry or the organization's relevant external environment; competition; technology; economic climate; market conditions; demographics; regulation; and, the quality of leadership.

As an organization nears maturity it needs to be alert to the fact that it may need to reinvent or renew itself (Point A in the figure above) before decline starts to set in (Point B in the figure above) to increase its chances of continuing to be viable.[3] Such a transition may necessitate the organization to refine its purpose.

Organizational units may also need to go through various evolutionary stages in their life cycle, calling for them to rethink their purpose. For example, an information technology department in a mid-sized bank I worked with saw the need to reinvent itself to optimize their contribution to their clients, the bank's various departments. As one IT manager put it," we need to get out of being an internal retail technology store". To initiate this needed value-added transition, we went to work on defining a new purpose for the IT department. Which was: "Enable departments to discover and implement technological innovations and solutions to improve their effectiveness and efficiency in achieving desired results". Following the strategic framework process, the leadership team then went on to create their new world through crafting a translatable vision, and forging a strategic path and resultant actions to make it happen. The biggest strategic shift was for IT professionals to get out of their offices and to form alliances with the departments they served and to really get to know their clients' respective businesses so that they could effectively collaborate on technological solutions and innovations.

The Value of Purpose

Purpose is the foundation from which everything flows. It alone enables an organization to develop a sound strategic direction and go to work. Unless the purpose is explicitly expressed and clearly understood and supported the organization is just reacting to events that occur.

The lack of a well-crafted purpose leads to a lack of unification and coordination throughout the organization. Decision makers will act on the basis of their different points of view, likely unaware of how doing so hurts the organization as a whole.

> I find images about common purpose very powerful. If you believe deep down that you and the others you work with have common purpose and values, you can still certainly pursue different objectives.
>
> Inevitably people will have different goals. But, if I really believe deep down that, in spite of these practical differences, we still have an enormous amount in common that we actually care about, then that changes my whole view. In that case I start to see myself and others less as separate beings, and more as parts of a greater whole.
>
> —Peter Senge
>
> Until thought is linked with purpose, there is no intelligent accomplishment.
>
> —James Allen

Guidelines for Defining Purpose

- The purpose statement should be short and sharply focused. It should be limited to a sentence.

- The purpose should state *why* the organization exists.

The *why* question is answered by first identifying just who the customer, client, or user is and just what it is that they find, or could find, of value or worth. It is okay to include in the purpose statement *what* the organization does and *how* it does it as long these additions make for a more powerful and meaningful purpose statement and help to clarify the *why*.

- The purpose should be far-reaching and timeless. It should be broad enough so as to not to restrict strategic thinking, yet specific enough to provide meaningful direction.

- The purpose needs to be clear and inspiring.

- "Making money" is not the purpose of an organization. Making money, or raising money, is a requirement. For if an organization does not generate the required amount of money, it will not be around to achieve its purpose. In addition, "making money" provides little organizational focus or direction. As Drucker points out, profitability is not the purpose of a business enterprise or activity, but a limiting factor. Profit is not the explanation, cause or rationale of business behavior and business decisions, but rather the test of validity.[4]

Examples of Purpose Statements

Below are a few examples of purpose statements for organizations you are familiar with.

> Enhance society by creating, collecting, and distributing high-specialty news, information, and entertainment.

> —The New York Times

17

To use our imagination to bring happiness to millions.

—Walt Disney Company

Provide you with the most useful and ethical financial services in the world.

—Charles Schwab

Organize the world's information and make it unusually accessible and useful.

—Google, Inc.

Below are a few examples of purpose statements from organizational units I have worked with.

Help employees better serve our customers and be more productive by providing technology solutions and access to needed information.

—Information Systems

Provide safe, clean facilities for children, families, and staff that support their quality of life and enhance the effectiveness of the agency's work.

—Facilities

Contribute to the ongoing success of the Business School by providing a continuous link for graduates and friends through quality programs and services.

—University Business Alumni Association

Assure that the general public, industrial, commercial, and residential customers understand and accept their responsibilities related to maintaining water quality and behave accordingly.

—Inspection

Create confident, competent young cooks armed with knowledge to make healthy food choices for life and share this knowledge with their friends and families.

—A nonprofit organization

Defining Your Purpose

Whether you are doing some initial quality thinking and hopefully interacting regarding your organization's purpose, or want to critically rethink your purpose, the questions below guide you through the process of crafting a powerful and meaningful purpose.

Remember that truly defining purpose is not easy. You may want to reflect on your work and come back to it several times before you are satisfied. You will also want to get constructive inputs from constituents.

The questions:

1. Who are our primary customers, clients, or users?

2. What is it that they find, or could find, of value or worth (the value proposition)?

3. If you think it makes for a more powerful and meaningful purpose statement and helps clarify the *why*, include a summary of *what* the organization does and/or *why* it does it.

4. After you have answered the questions above to your satisfaction, pull the elements together to form a well-worded, powerful, one-sentence summary that captures why your organization exists.

Test your draft by asking yourself the following questions:

- Does the purpose statement summarize what the primary customers, clients, or users finds, or could find, of value or worth?

- If the what we do and/or how we do it are included in the statement, do the additions enhance the power and meaningfulness of the statement and help to clarify the why?

- Is the purpose statement far-reaching and timeless?

- Do I get a "fire in the belly" when I reflect on the statement? How about a little "tingle"? If not, it's time to do some additional quality thinking about what you are up to or your depiction of its utility.

3

CLARIFYING CORE VALUES: WHAT DO WE STAND FOR?

To act with integrity, you must know who you are—what you stand for, and what you believe in, what you care most about.

Mastery of the art of leadership comes from mastery of the self. It's about leading out of what is already in your soul.

—James Kouzes and Barry Posner,
The Leadership Challenge

Establish IDENTITY

"Why do we exist?"
"What do we stand for?"
- **Purpose**
- **Core Values**

What Are Core Values?

Core Values   Essential and enduring beliefs based on key business ideas that guide the everyday thinking and behavior of an organization.

The Power of Shared Values[1]

The route to commitment begins by clarifying personal values. However, the greatest accomplishments are possible when both leaders and constituents share common values. Research clearly shows that people are more committed to the organization when clear, strong values are shared. Shared values make a difference in work attitudes and performance.

Shared values make a difference because they:

- Foster strong feeling of personal effectiveness.
- Promote high levels of organizational loyalty.
- Facilitate consensus about key organizational goals and stakeholders.
- Encourage ethical behavior.
- Promote strong norms about working hard and caring.
- Reduce levels of job stress and tension.
- Foster pride in the organization.
- Facilitate understanding about performance expectations.
- Foster teamwork and esprit de corps.

Shared values are the glue that holds people together in good times and bad.

In good times, shared values are a common language for expressing standards and ambitions. In more troubled times, they can be the beacon that lights the way.

Make Your Values Mean Something

As delineated above, values can be extremely valuable to an organization. Values help clarify an organization's identity and serve as a rallying point for employees. But coming up with strong core values and living them requires leadership discipline and fortitude.

Values statements need to mean something. Empty values statements can create cynical and dispirited employees. But creating and living strong values requires leadership and organizational discipline.

If a leader is not willing to develop and live strong values *based on key business ideas* it is better off to not go through the motions.

The word *core* is used in conjunction with values because the values need to be few in number. Certainly, no more than five. They are few in number because they are based on key business ideas that lie at the heart of an organization's identity. They are both essential and enduring. Patrick Lencioni describes core values as those timeless beliefs that manically drive an organization.[2]

Lencioni identifies and defines other types of values in addition to core values. They are:

Permission-to-play values   These are the minimal behavioral standards required of an organization. Although they are important, they do not serve to clarify or differentiate the organization from others. These are for example values such as honesty and respect for others.

Accidental values	These traits are evident in an organization but have come accidentally and do not necessarily serve the organization well. For example, hiring people with similar backgrounds, socio-economic status, world views, or personal style.
Aspirational values	These are characteristics that an organization thinks it must develop to optimize its success. Although such values may be desirable, they should not be confused with core values that do not change over time and do not come and go with the needs of the business.

An understanding of the different kinds of values helps an organization from diluting the core. Core values are what matter the most.[3]

Values and Culture

Culture is the way an organization goes about its business and the way its people behave with one another and constituents, be they customers, suppliers, regulators, visitors, or the public. An organization's culture is its character.

Every organization has a culture, either by design or default. That being the case, it makes good sense for an organization to be intentional about building a culture that uniquely fits its business and will help sustain success through thick and thin. And the way to go about building an appropriate, vibrant culture tailored to the organization is through developing and living core values based on the organization's key business ideas. Core values are the underpinnings of a culture.

24

And if an organization found the need to change it's culture, which is no small undertaking, it first needs to make sure it has a set of core values that supports the change.

Guidelines for Developing Core Values

1. *Values clarification starts with the leader.* Whether that is the leader of the organization as a whole or an organizational unit. *The leader needs to find, express, and model his or her voice.*

   In a larger organization a single set of core values may not provide enough specific and behavioral guidance for the various organizational units throughout the organization. In such cases, with the approval of the organization as a whole, various organizational units may need to develop their own set of core values or tailor the operating definitions of shared organizational values to specifically fit their needs. Doing so should be encouraged as long as the subunit's core values align with and support the core values of the organization as a whole.

   For you as the leader start with your own important personal values. Think about which of these values might be appropriate work values for your organization. Next think about the critical work values for your organization based on key business ideas. Your personal value or values may come into play.

   Express core values in just a word or two using an appropriate modifier to make for a clear, compelling label for each core value. For example, the core values for a small professional consulting group were: Collaborative Partnering; Rapid Response; and Earned Credibility. You can use more than one or two words, but aim to be concise.

25

The key question is: *"What are those essential and enduring beliefs based on key business ideas that will serve as strong and timeless thinking and behavioral guides for the organization?"*

2. *Involve your leadership team in a genuine and meaningful way in identifying and clarifying core values.* This does not mean that values creation should be a democratic process. In fact, in most cases it is preferable that it is not.

In considering the various decision-making options to use in working with your leadership team, the consultative mode is the best option. Refer to Figure 1.3, Leader Decision-Making Options, in chapter 1.

Your goal is to have the core values become shared values. Quality engagement with your leadership team is a positive step in achieving this goal. Involvement breeds ownership.

If you are open to the idea of being aware of what the individual members of your team think the core values should be, you are encouraged to get their individual inputs. In doing so it is important that you are genuine in your desire to hear from them. Otherwise, it will just be a perfunctory exercise, hurting your credibility.

Getting individual inputs before sharing what you think the core values should be can be valuable both to you and the team. It involves them in the process and paves the way to have a fruitful dialogue regarding potential core values. You may even see fit to amend your current list of core values. And a rich dialogue will pay dividends when it comes to the next step—crafting an operating definition for each of the core values.

Use the process below as an effective and efficient way of obtaining individual inputs and then converting the individual inputs to a collective product.

Obtaining Individual Team Member
Core Values Inputs

This process is an adaptation of the use of the Affinity Diagram. See Appendix A for a detailed description of the Affinity Diagram.

Setting the Stage

a. Assure that the team members understand what core values are and the integral role they play in developing an organization's identity.

b. Explain that you have already engaged in quality reflective thinking on the subject and have come up with a draft of the critical few core values you think represent essential and enduring believes that are instrumental for guiding everyday organizational thinking and behavior.

   Explain that clarifying core values needs to start with the leader. The leader must truly believe in the core values if they are going to be useful. And that the leader needs to model the way. Core values need to be lived.

   Explain that you want to share your current list of core values, but would first like to get inputs from the individual team members. To do so, state that a practical and proven process will be used to obtain individual inputs, and then the team members will work together to develop a collective list of core values.

Explain that you will then share your current list of core values and engage in genuine dialogue to determine the final list of core values. Emphasize that in arriving at a final list of core values that you, as leader, still need to remain the primary decider when it comes to core values.

The Process

c. Give each team member five 3"x5" 3M Post-It™ notes. Explain that you are limiting the number because we are trying to identify *core* values. Also provide each member with a black Sharpie pen.

d. Have each team member summarize on a note in a word or few words any input they have for a core value. One core value per note, up to a maximum of five core values. No need to come up with five.

e. After the individuals have completed their work, have them post the notes to sheets of flipchart paper on a wall or on a table.

f. The only discussion at this time is to allow for any questions of clarification as to what has been posted.

g. Have the team members sort the notes into logical clusters.

h. Have the team members come up with the best core value label for each cluster.

i. Share your current list of core values. Engage the team in a meaningful dialogue regarding potential core values.

j. If feasible, agree on a list of core values. Realize that you may want to keep the list open to change for now. Views may change once you go on and develop an operating definition for each of the core values. You also may want to allow some time to go out and live the values before sharing them with the organization as a whole.

k. Thank the team for their inputs.

3. *Each value needs to be clearly and specifically defined* to allow for a shared understanding with each member of the leadership. And subsequently with the organization as a whole. You need to engage your leadership work in quality thinking and interacting in defining your core values.

The recommended structure for articulating and eventually communicating your core values is shown in Figure 3.1 below.

Figure 3.1 Structure for Articulating Core Values

Value	Definition
Use a word or two to create a clear, compelling label for each core value. Choose modifiers to have the value stand on its own and avoid misinterpretation.	*Use a sentence or several sentences to operationally define the value. How is it manifested in doing our work? Use common language and, if it helps, include colloquialisms and metaphors to create meaningful symbolism.*

See the examples below to help you understand clarifying core values and the utility of using the recommended structure.

Our Core Values
(What We Stand For)

Value	Definition
• _____	_____. _____
	_____. _____
	_____.
• _____	_____. _____
	_____. _____
	_____.
• _____	_____. _____
	_____. _____
	_____.

Examples of Core Values

Toyota

Value	Definition
Respect for People	*Respect* Respect others, make every effort to understand each other, take responsibility, and do our best to build mutual trust.
	Teamwork We stimulate personal and professional growth, share opportunities of development, and maximize individual and team performance.

| Continuous Improvement | *Challenge*
We form a long-term vision, meeting challenges with courage and creativity to realize our dreams. |
| | |

Challenge

We form a long-term vision, meeting challenges with courage and creativity to realize our dreams.

Kaizen (Continuous Improvement)
We improve our business operations continuously, always driving for innovation and evolution.

Genchi Genbutsu (Go and see for yourself)
We go to the source to find the facts to make correct decisions, build consensus, and achieve our goals.

From a corporate Human Resources department

Value	Definition
Strategic Partner	Our success in providing quality human resources advice and service to our various department clients is directly related to how well we know each of their businesses. We also need to continue to cultivate effective working relationships. Doing these things allows us to collaborate with them to tailor strategies and solutions to help them effectively manage their current realities and anticipate or respond to their unique emerging opportunities and challenges.
Professionalism	We need to be totally professional in everything we do. This includes continually being abreast of the latest research and developments in our field; conducting ourselves in an exemplary manner.

Assessing Buy-In

The leadership team has to have a shared understanding of the core values and genuinely support them if they are going to have a chance of becoming part of the organizational fabric and be lived throughout the organization. For like you, the leader, your team has to model the way.

After you and your leadership team have engaged in quality thinking and interacting leading to the identification of the values and an operating definition of each it is time to assess just how much agreement and support genuinely exists amongst the members of your leadership team for the values before moving on.

Figure 3.2 describes methods for testing for agreement.

Figure 3.2 Testing for Agreement

Speculate	Speculate that it seems that consensus has been reached. Observe the reaction to the statement. Invite feedback.
Individual Polling	Ask each team member if she or he can support the decision being proposed.
Gradients of Agreement Scale	Poll the team using the Gradients of Agreement methodology described below.

Given the importance of knowing just how much each of the members of your leadership genuinely supports the values, it is highly recommended that you use the *Gradients of Agreement Scale* as detailed in Appendix B to make such an assessment. It is an extremely effective way to determine the degree of support that exists from each of your team members. And if there are concerns, to surface them and deal with them.

The process of value creation cannot and should not be rushed. No matter how well you and your leadership team have reached consensus and buy-in regarding your core values, you want to see how they play out in everyday life and be willing to make modifications. Once you and your leadership team are satisfied that your core values truly capture the essence of what you stand for, they will be fairly constant over time. But you and your team need to be continually vigilant to ensure that your core values continue to represent the organization's essential and enduring beliefs based on key business ideas in the context of your relevant external and internal environments.

Living Your Values

Regardless of the quality, acceptance, and relevance of the core values you have identified and defined, they are only words until you and your leadership team, and your organization begin to live them.

Once you and your leadership team have fully embraced the values you need to share them with the rest of the organization. In so doing, resist the temptation of just rolling them out as so many organizations do. As previously stated regarding implementing your sound strategy as a whole, roll outs do not work.

Also resist the temptation of producing wallet cards and posters, at least for the time being. Instead, you and your leadership team need face-to-face conversations to enhance the understanding and acceptance of the values and how they bolster organizational effectiveness. For larger organizations, such quality conversations then need to cascade down through the organization.

Simultaneously and continually, you and your leadership team need to model the way. This is critical. You model the way by both "talking the talk" and "walking the walk".

Model the Way—Talking the Talk

Borrowing from a book by Terry Pearce, you talk the talk by *Leading Out Loud*[4] to clarify values and inspire commitment. In communicating the values, you of course will talk about the content of the values, what Ron Crossland, in his book, *Voice Lessons, Applying Science to the Art of Leadership Communication*[5], calls the factual channel of communication. Speaking from the head. But to enhance understanding, acceptance, and commitment you also need to make use of what he calls the emotional channel. That is, feelings. Both your feelings and your perceived feelings of your audience. Speaking from the heart. And, also to use the symbolic channel. That is, stories, examples, and metaphors, to make the values come alive and resonate with your audience. Crossland argues that people, especially leaders, need to develop skills in using all three channels. Using all three channels is of great value in attempting to communicate important messages, especially when resistance may be a factor. The content is of course important, but you do not want to rely solely on this channel in attempting to communicate important messages.

Crossland's valuable advice, that is, using all three communication channels, (factual, emotional, and symbolic) in communicating as a leader is bolstered by Chip Heath and Dan Heath in their book *Make It Stick*.[6] One of the key messages they emphasize in using the factual channel is to make sure your *intent* is clear. For example, making sure the business rationale for each of the core values is clear. A well-worded definition of the core value should accomplish this. When people know the intent, they are more likely to align their behaviors with the values as they live them.

Model the Way——Walking the Talk

You walk the talk by aligning your actions and your talk with the core values you believe in and want your organization to live. You model the way by making the values part of your everyday life. You *operationalize* them.

Below are some of the ways you can operationalize your core values.

- *How you spend your time and what you pay attention to* is the clearest indicator of the degree the values are important to you. The behaviors of leaders send clear messages of what they think is important.

- *Critical incidents* present teaching moments for you as a leader. Critical incidents provide opportunities to demonstrate what is valued and what is not.

- Values can be reinforced by incorporating them into the organization's *management systems*, such as strategy formulation and execution; performance measurement; and workforce management systems such as staffing, onboarding, performance management, reward and recognition, and training and development.

- *Communicate examples and stories* about how people used the values in achieving desired results.

- Using the values to help guide problem solving and decision making.

4

IDENTIFYING DISTINCT CORE CAPABILITIES: IS THERE ANYTHING WE ARE UNIQUELY REALLY GOOD AT?

....

> To understand the value-creating potential of organizations and people, one must first understand the identity that is at their core
>
> —Lawrence Ackerman,
> *Identity Is Destiny*

An organization's purpose (who we are) and core values (what we stand for) constitute its identity. The last two chapters discussed each of these components of identity, and how to engage in in quality thinking and interacting to identify and define these factors that are unique to your organization.

But there is another possible factor that is important for an organization to honestly attempt to discover and utilize to help it to establish its identity and set its direction. I use the phrase "honestly attempt to discover" because this factor may not exist for an organization, at least not yet. Or maybe never.

This factor is any distinct core capabilities an organization has. Whether the organization is in the start-up stage of its organizational evolution, or well into its growth stage. If any such distinct core capabilities do indeed exist, they should be used to help define the organization's identity and help it architect its direction.

What Are Distinct Core Capabilities?

Distinct Core Capabilities   The basketful of people and process know-how that may exist in an organization that distinguishes it and allows it to achieve sustainable results in its marketplace or relevant external environment. Distinct core capabilities answer the question: "What are we really good at?"[1]

Some key points about distinct core capabilities are discussed below.

Distinct core capabilities:

- Are about "know-how", and not about physical assets. Unlike physical assets, distinct core capabilities do not deteriorate as they are shared and applied. On the contrary, they grow.

  Physical assets, including monetary resources, may provide an organization with a leg up or be the means for a short-term advantage. But unless they are backed up by a sound strategy and the capability to deliver, the organization will surely lose the advantage such assets once provided.

- Must provide a sustainable competitive advantage in an organization's market place or relevant external environment. Distinct core capabilities are difficult for competitors to imitate.

- Need to make a significant contribution to the value proposition for the customer. That is, the "what the customer/client/user finds, or could find, of value or use", as discussed in chapter 2.

37

- Are not, as discussed earlier, present in all organizations. This is not necessarily a slap in the face to the organization. Perhaps the organization does not yet have a track record and distinct core capabilities have yet to surface or mature. Perhaps the organization is in a commodity business. Or perhaps, it just does not have any such capabilities.

- Unless they genuinely have external or internal competition, distinct core capabilities do not typically exist in organizational units, as contrasted with the organization as a whole. There is no need for these internal units to necessarily develop and sustain a competitive advantage.

- Just as with purpose and core values, to truly be distinct core capabilities they must be far-reaching and timeless. They are a part of the organization's fabric and stand a good chance of being so for a long time. But it is important for an organization to not rest on its laurels, but to continue to nurture and grow such capabilities, and perhaps make necessary changes and mutations to address emerging realities for the organization.

Example of Distinct Core Capabilities[2]

Organization and Industry	Distinct Core Capabilities
Applied Materials *Semiconductor equipment*	Rapid high-technology product development and rollout.
	Rapid production/delivery of highly customized product.

Cooper Tire *Replacement auto and truck tires*	Low-cost product design and manufacturing along with continual cost control and reduction.
Sun Microsystems *Workstations*	Rapid high-technology product development and rollout.
	Operational flexibility.
Motorola *Semiconductors and electrical equipment*	Continuous quality improvement.
	Rapid high-technology product development and rollout.
	Operational flexibility

Your Organization

If you currently have ay distinct core capabilities as we have defined them here, go about identifying and defining them. Then determine how they can help you better define your purpose, your core values, and help you set a viable direction.

II

FORMULATING STRATEGY: DIRECTION

Part I discussed the importance and process for establishing an Identity. An Identity consisting of a powerfully worded, compelling one-sentence purpose that avers why the organization exists; and the critical few core values that clearly state what the organization stands for.

The Identity serves as the organization's foundation from which to set its Direction for creating its future.

Chapter 5 speaks to the importance of trying to visualize the big dream for the organization. The ultimate quest that serves as the north star to guide the organization on its ongoing journey. Chapter 6 shows you how to logically go about assessing what is going on in the organization's current relevant external environment so you can identify the critical areas of strategic focus that propel you toward that quest. Next, you need to assess the organization's capability to address the strategic focus.

Chapter 7 shows you how to craft a translatable, interim vision based on your strategic focus. An actionable vision that focuses on an appropriate planning horizon for you and allows you to construct a strategic path, the subject of Chapter 8, that allows you to forge ahead.

Chapter 9 discusses going about planning actions to achieve the strategies that comprise your strategic path. It includes a practical and proven format for constructing action plans to get the job done.

5

IMAGINING YOUR BIG DREAM: WHAT IS OUR ULTIMATE QUEST?

The journey of 1,000 miles starts with a single step.

—Lao-tzu

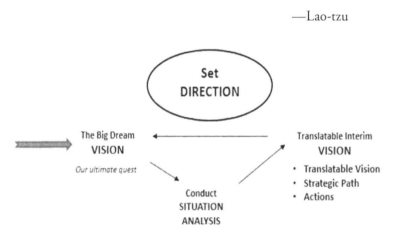

A good place to start envisioning your future is to dream big and think far off into the future. Such a dream represents your ultimate quest. It is a big and bold inspiration to provide or contribute something bigger than yourself for the common good. The common good of society, the community, or customers/clients/users. It may be unattainable, yet still serves as your north star in providing continuous guidance for your journey, perhaps a long and arduous journey, but one that will hopefully be exciting and rewarding.

The WHY of the organization is answered by its purpose (why we exist) and its big dream (the ultimate reason for why we do what we do).[1]

President Kennedy's big dream and challenge for NASA was to land a man on the moon. And it turned out to be "a giant step for mankind". Martin Luther King's big dream elucidated in his famous and moving "I Have a Dream" speech was for genuine equality to exist. Progress has been made toward fulfilling that dream, but there is still a long way to go.

Your big dream as a leader may not be as big or bold as going to the moon, but perhaps you do have an inspiration bigger than yourself that you and your organization can contribute to over time with its identity and direction.

To give an example. A behavioral health organization I worked with had an interim vision of building a health care system that connects and integrates the diverse elements of a behavioral health system for the benefit of all involved in the system. Their ultimate or big dream vision was to provide organizations with a comprehensive and proven set of solutions for the effective management of the human resource factor.

If you cannot currently imagine a big inspirational dream beyond yourself that you and your organization can contribute to, don't fret. Perhaps you will imagine such a quest as you work through the Strategic Framework in the near term or as time goes by. Maybe not. In any case, using the Strategic Framework to formulate and execute a sound strategy will serve you well.

6

CONDUCTING A SITUATION ANALYSIS: WHAT IS GOING ON IN OUR RELEVANT EXTERNAL AND INTERNAL ENVIRONMENTS?

Probably the most dangerous and fallacious of all hidden assumptions in business models is that today will be the same as tomorrow and every day thereafter.

—Winslow Ferrell

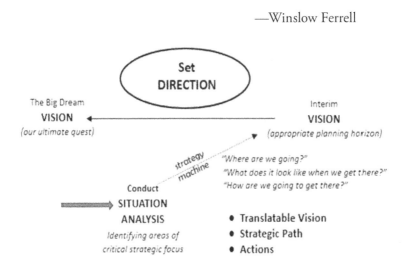

What Is a Situation Analysis?

Before crafting an interim, translatable vision and resultant strategic path and actions, it makes sense to get your bearings. Just what is going on in your relevant world? Conducting a situation analysis or environmental scan allows you to answer this important question in a logical, comprehensive, and inclusive manner.

Situation Analysis	A process to enable a leadership team to engage in quality thinking and interacting to identify the critical few areas of strategic focus the organization needs to concentrate on to create its desired future.

The four questions that need to be answered in conducting a situation analysis are:

- *"What is going on in our relevant external environment?"*

- *Based on what is going on in our relevant external environment, "What are the critical few areas of strategic focus for us in creating our desired future?"*

- *"What is our current organizational capability to constructively address these critical opportunities or challenges?"*

- *"Are there any organizational capability opportunities or challenges that also represent a critical area of strategic focus?"*

Conducting a situation analysis before getting on with creating your future provides many valuable benefits. They include:

- Allowing you and your leadership team, and possibly other constituents, to get on the same page as to just what is going on in your relevant external environment that needs attention and your organizational capability to do so.

- Identifying planning assumptions or premises.

- Discovering trends and developing insights.

Factor Analysis

Perhaps you and your leadership team can just have a discussion to identify and describe your critical few areas of strategic focus. Perhaps not. At least not in a comprehensive way, and a way that allows all the team members to have an equal chance to input, and their inputs understood.

That is the beauty of the Factor Analysis methodology described below. Identifying your critical few areas for strategic focus is just too important to leave to chance.

Factor Analysis is a much more rigorous and complete process than the popular SWOT Analysis that is intended for the same purpose. The components of a SWOT Analysis are **S**trengths and **W**eaknesses (internal factors) and **O**pportunities and **T**hreats (external factors). It is a good tool, but a factor analysis will just do a better job for you.

The steps in conducting a factor analysis are the following:

1. Acknowledge any preconditions.[1]

    Before launching into any kind of intelligence gathering and analysis, it is important to determine if there are any relevant preconditions. That is, to surface any management commitments or organizational limitations that have a bearing on your team's strategic thinking and planning. Acknowledging and addressing any such preconditions at the outset minimizes the chances of disruption late on in your planning process.

2. Identify and analyze relevant external environmental factors.

    a. Identify relevant external environmental factors.

Typical external factors for the *organization as a whole* include such considerations as:

- customers/clients/users
- stakeholders
- suppliers
- marketplace dynamics
- the industry
- competition
- the community

- trade allies
- technology
- regulations
- economic conditions
- social changes
- demographics
- the labor market

In addition to the factors above, *organizational units* need to include "direction from above" as an external factor in that such direction is external to their specific organizational unit.

Use the above as a guide to develop your own list of relevant external environmental factors for your organization.

b. Gather and analyze relevant intelligence.

Gathering and analyzing relevant intelligence related to some or all of the factors you have identified and want to consider can range from simple to quite involved. The uniqueness, complexity, and importance of a factor being considered and the kind of assessment you think you need to do will influence your intelligence gathering.

For each factor you need to determine what intelligence would be valuable to have; how to go about obtaining it; and the depth and breadth of your search from a cost-benefit perspective.

Forms of intelligence gathering may include such activities as stakeholder, customer, and employee inputs; competitor data; financial data; and, the identification of important trends. You of course will also want to tap into other resources, both inside and outside the organization that may be useful in your analysis.

The good news is that in most instances the needed intelligence resides within your team. You can tap into such intelligence when you gather your team to conduct your situation analysis. You can also make assignments to specific team members in advance advance of the situation analysis to gather specific intelligence and be prepared to discuss when you get together. A one-page summary of the intelligence gathered is a useful practice. It is also most times advantageous to have such summaries distributed in advance with instructions to the team to review the summaries and come prepared to discuss when your team meets.[2]

3. Decide on the critical few areas of strategic focus.

    a. With your team, for each external factor considered, discuss anything of relevance to your analysis that is occurring in that factor. Make use of any intelligence gathered in advance and the related summaries in doing so. Specifically identify any specific opportunities or challenges that need to be considered. For this purpose, it is recommended that you use a sheet of flipchart paper for each external factor. List the specific opportunities or challenges for that factor on the sheet of paper. Be brief and precise in your wording. Use a single sentence to define just what the opportunity or challenge is. Such opportunities or challenges represent the potential areas of strategic focus for you and your team.

Repeat the process of identifying potential areas of strategic focus for each of the external factors that you are considering.

Ensure that all team members completely understand each potential area of strategic focus, and why it is thought to be important.

b. Your goal now is to reduce these potential areas of strategic focus to the *critical few*. The key here, as is the case with all your strategic thinking and planning, is focus, focus, focus. You can only work on so much at a time. So, make it count.

The critical areas of strategic focus selected will form the elements for your interim, translatable vision, the next step in the strategy formulation process, and the subject of the next chapter.

Review the critical areas of strategic focus and *synthesize* any potential areas that logically go together. Reword the opportunity or challenge if necessary to reflect the synthesis.

To optimize individual input and decision making consider using dot stickers to allow each member to weigh in on the potential areas of strategic focus identified and described. Give each team member six green dot stickers to indicate their choices for the most important areas of focus for them. More than one dot can be used for a specific area of potential focus. Also, give each member two red dot stickers to indicate what, if any, may be areas that may seem to be important but may represent an area of distraction or something that the organization cannot do anything about in the near future. The team's green dots will signify what it thinks are the areas of critical strategic focus.[2]

Review and discuss the results of the team's analysis. Use the results to determine your critical areas of strategic focus. Assure that you did not put too much on your plate. More than six areas of focus may be too many. Some areas of potential strategic focus may just need to be delayed for now. Other areas, although they are important, may not rise to the level of being a strategic priority and can be dealt with in the course of normal business.

Remember that you as the leader have the final say.

4. Assess organizational capability

In planning from the outside in, the importance of which has been previously stressed, you have identified and defined your organization's critical areas of strategic focus. Next you need to assess your organization's capability to constructively address these opportunities and challenges.

Structure 6.1 describes the building blocks of organizational capability that you can use to assess your organization's readiness to address the external areas of critical strategic focus that you have identified and described.

Figure 6.1 Organizational Capability Building Blocks

Building Block (Internal Factor)	Description
Sound Strategy	Clear, compelling definition of why the organization exists (its identity); where it is going (its vision); and how it plans to get there (its strategic path).

Structure   The arranging and relating of work to optimize the accomplishment of the sound strategy. Includes organization design; use of teams; plant and equipment; policies, practices, and procedures.

Systems   The design and use of useful mechanisms to effectively and efficiently accomplish the sound strategy.

Management systems, such as strategy formulation and execution; budgeting; and performance measurement. *Operating systems,* such as financial, marketing, procurement, marketing, procurement, production, and customer service. *Human systems,* such as staffing; performance management, reward and recognition; and training and development.

Workforce   The competence and commitment of people to use the
Capability   systems and operate within the structure to achieve desired results.

With your team use the organizational building blocks to engage in quality thinking and interacting to assess your organizational readiness to constructively address the critical few external areas of strategy focus that you have identified and described from your analysis thus far.

If you identify potential areas of internal strategic focus that you consider to be critical to formulating a sound strategy, consider adding to your existing list of external critical areas of strategic focus. Reassess the total list. Is your revised list manageable? Do you need to postpone any areas of strategic focus, if indeed they can wait?

Figure 6.3 Identifying the Critical Few Areas of Strategic Focus

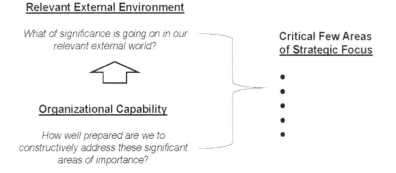

Discussed below are two methodologies you may want to consider to supplement your team's factor analysis work.

Scenario Planning

Scenario planning is a method for identifying future possibilities that may occur in your relevant external environment and the impact they might have on your organization. Scenario planning is "what if" planning.

Identifying and discussing such possible scenarios exposes your organization's business assumptions. Doing so is different than forecasting, which rarely challenges the assumptions beneath the forecast.

Scenarios should be constructed around key uncertainties that might have huge impacts on your organization. They should be broad and diverse in nature. They can be both positive ("best case") or pessimistic ("worst case") relative to your environment in general or to specific factors.

If you gain any significant insights from using scenario planning, revisit the areas of critical strategic focus you have identified, both external and internal, to see if you need to make any adjustments to effectively address or incorporate any of these assumptions into your planning.

Scenario planning, if used, should not be a one-time event. Or used only when developing or updating your sound strategy. Rather such planning should be used as an ongoing organizational learning process to update your strategic assumptions relative to your real world.

Distinct Core Capabilities

The concept of distinct core capabilities was discussed in chapter 2 when we looked at defining purpose. As discussed then, distinct core capabilities, if you have any, are not a part of purpose. They are a "What" and not a "Why". But it sometimes useful to see how such core capabilities may fit into either your purpose or your strategic thinking or planning, especially any internal areas critical strategic focus you may have identified.

CRAFTING AN INTERIM, TRANSLATABLE VISION: WHERE ARE WE GOING? WHAT DOES IT LOOK LIKE WHEN WE GET THERE?

The best way to predict the future is to create it.

—Albert Einstein

One day Alice came to a fork in the road and saw a Cheshire cat in a tree. "Which road do I take?" she asked. His response was a question: "Where do you want to go?" "I don't know," Alice answered. "Then", said the cat, "It doesn't matter".

—Lewis Carroll,
Alice in Wonderland

Let's start off with the definition of vision.

Vision   A unique, positive, and compelling image of the future for the common good.

A vision shares the same qualities as purpose.

It is *unique*. It comes from within. It is a belief. It is not something that is copied.

It is *positive*. It is something to be desired.

It is *compelling*. It stirs the emotions. It motivates.

It is for the *common good*; not for just a chosen few.

The difference is that purpose defines why the organization exists. Whereas vision states where the organization wants and needs to go.

The Need for an Actionable Vision

As discussed, if you have a big dream it serves as your north star in directing you toward your ultimate quest. If you don't, that's okay. One may become evident later.

But whether or not you have a big dream, you need to craft a vision that specifically articulates your desired future state for the near term so you can get to work on making it happen. Most visions are too abstract to fulfill this purpose. But you can craft such a vision by making use of the situation analysis you and your team conducted. The opportunities and challenges identified and described can be incorporated into your vision as elements in the form of desired results, making for an actionable vision. These desired results allow you to identify resultant strategies, and eventually actions, to propel you forward to create your desired future state.

Crafting such an interim translatable vision allows you to specifically define your new reality.

An interim translatable vision answers the questions:

- Where are we going?
- What does it look like when we get there?

I am indebted to my colleague Allan McCarthy for his wisdom and insight in developing this valuable leadership concept of a translatable vision and its structure, the details of which we will describe in a bit.[1]

The Power of Vision

> If any one idea has inspired organizations for thousands of years, it's the capability to hold a shared picture of the future we seek to create.
>
> —Peter Senge

The real power of a vision is not what it says, but what it does. When clearly articulated and shared, a vision, along with a genuine desire to bring it into reality, is a powerful force. A well-crafted and shared vision enhances effectiveness and motivation through the omnipresent creative tension that exists between the desired future state and the current reality. Just by articulating a powerful vision all kinds of possibilities open up. Opportunities for moving forward are identified that you would not have otherwise discovered. This phenomenon can be called "cultivating serendipity". Once you have described just what you want to see, you will begin to see what you have described. Read this last sentence again. It is profound.

Guidelines for Crafting a Vision

- *Identify an appropriate planning horizon* for your organization. Although not as necessarily timeless as purpose, a vision needs to be *far reaching*. But just how far reaching? There is no hard-and-fast rule as to how far into the future a leader needs to look. An appropriate planning horizon is determined by many variables. Such variables as the nature of your industry and business; the stage of your organization in its evolution, as described in chapter 2; the leader's hierarchical level in the organization; and a variety of other factors in your relevant external environment, as discussed in Chapter 6. Three to five years seems to be an appropriate planning horizon for most organizations.

Regardless of the time span of your planning horizon, working to achieve a vision needs to be thought of as a journey, not a destination. Like any worthwhile and difficult journey, there will be bends in the road, plateaus, and obstacles to overcome. Your strategic path and actions to move you toward your vision will no doubt be modified to address emerging opportunities and challenges. And as you get closer to achieving your current interim vision, you will want to architect a new interim vision to help guide you toward your ultimate quest. Think of working to achieve your vision, or series of visions, as an organic process rather than a mechanical one.

- *Use the critical few areas of strategic focus* you identified by conducting your situation analysis as the foundation for crafting your vision.

- To optimize its usefulness, a vision needs to be *actionable* or *translatable*. A well-crafted vision allows for backwards planning. It is like planting a stake in the ground and working backward to determine how best to get there. Your strategic path and actions to propel you toward your vision should flow directly from the vision elements formulated from your critical areas of strategic focus.

Process for Crafting an Interim Translatable Vision

A translatable vision is comprised of two parts—a vision statement and vision elements.

- The **vision statement** is a fifteen- to thirty-word summary of the vision. It is an overarching or umbrella statement that captures the essence of the desired future state.

- The **vision elements** are statements that summarize the conditions or evidences that exist when the vision statement is achieved. They are compelling one-sentence statements of the specific results that will be achieved by successfully working on the critical few areas of strategic focus identified by the situation analysis.

  The vision elements answer the question: "How do we know success when we see it?" In addition, the vision elements provide the needed specificity to facilitate the forging of a logical resultant strategic path and actions. Hence, constituting a translatable or actionable vision.

An Example

From the information systems department of a bank:

VISION

Vision Statement	Partner with the bank's departments to effectively design and implement appropriate information technology strategies that enable them to constructively address business opportunities and challenges.

We will be successful in achieving this vision when:

Vision
Elements

- A department environment and staff and vendor capability exist that significantly contribute to the bank's success by staying on the forefront of technology development and fostering a sense of pride and personal growth.

- An innovative and operational infrastructure is designed, built, and operated that effectively supports the bank's current and future business activities by utilizing the industry's best practices.

- Timely technical ideas and solutions are provided by collaborating with all levels of the organization on strategic business opportunities and challenges.

- Timely, user-friendly service to all employees is provided by seeking opportunities to help them utilize or implement technology-based solutions that improve their business processes and enhance their computer skills.

Most often it works best for a strategic planning team to start by articulating the vision elements. Then after describing what the desired future state looks like, to craft a vision statement that captures the essence of what the future state looks like. But it can work either way. Do what you think will work best for you.

Articulating Vision Elements

<u>What to Do</u>

1. Agree on the critical areas of strategic focus identified by your situation analysis. Be sure and synthesize similar areas of focus to help keep things manageable. More than six areas of focus is too many.

2. Expand your notations of areas of critical focus into full one-sentence result statements, as illustrated by the example

above. Do so by mentally prefacing each statement with the word *when* since these statements represent the conditions that exist *when* your future desired state is achieved.

Articulating a Vision Statement

Your vision statement is a one-sentence summary that captures the essence of your desired future state, as delineated by your vision elements. It is an overarching or umbrella statement.

<u>What to Do</u>

1. Reflect on the draft of your vision elements and search for common themes that may be woven throughout.

2. Use the structure below to help you articulate your vision statement.

Figure 7.1 Basic Components of a Vision Statement[2]

Objective	Ends	The ultimate objective that will drive the operation of the business over the next several years (the planning horizon).
Scope	Domain	As applicable, the boundaries that help define which areas of activities to concentrate on.
		Dimensions to consider: • Target customers • Offerings • Geographical location(s) • Horizontal integration • Vertical integration
Advantage	Means	Our unique capability or activities that will allow us to deliver the value proposition to our customers/clients/users.

8

CHARTING A STRATEGIC PATH: HOW ARE WE GOING TO GET THERE?

We can either direct the process of goals and actions to lead us to where we really want to go, or we can just drift along unfocused.

—Source unknown

A vision without action is but a dream; action without vision is a waste of time; but vision with action can change our lives.

—M. Ignacio Tinajero

Where You Are

On the road so far traveled you have gained important insights, and after engaging in quality thinking and interacting, have articulated the essence of your organization (purpose) and your essential and enduring beliefs that provide daily behavioral guidance (core values). Likewise, you have gained insights regarding just what is going on in your relevant external environment and your capability to constructively address the critical few areas of strategic focus you have identified (situation analysis). You have used your analysis to succinctly and powerfully describe your desired future state (interim translatable vision). Now it is time to move from insight to action. To chart a strategic path to move you toward achieving your vision.

What Is a Strategic Path?

Strategic Path	The critical few strategic initiatives that are essential to propel the organization toward achieving its vision.

The words *critical few* have been used repeatedly as we have walked through the strategy formulation process. We use the words here once again. The words are used repeatedly to help you incorporate a key tenet of effective strategy formulation into your strategic thinking—focus, focus, focus. That is what strategy formulation is all about. And to focus you have to make decisions, sometimes very tough decisions, to narrow things down to what is important and manageable. The things that are important to concentrate your limited time and resources on in the near future with a view toward the distant future to optimize your organizational effectiveness. It is the application of the Pareto Law or Principle (also known as the 80/20 Principle). This principle posits that 80% of the results come from 20% of the activities. That an unequal relationship exists between inputs and outputs. Whether that be with regard to wealth, human resources, profits, and a variety of other phenomenon. Let's not quibble about the percentage. And unlike other principles, the Pareto Principle is not a law. It is merely an observation. And it certainly does not apply to every scenario. But it does apply to many situations. And, it is certainly relevant when it comes to strategy formulation[*]

Artist's Rendering Is Not Enough

Allan McCarthy uses a great analogy to stress the importance of the leadership team going beyond crafting a vision in the strategy formulation process. The analogy is about the design and construction of a custom-built home.[1]

---

[*] Vilfredo Pareto was an esteemed 19th century Italian economist. He derived the principle from observing the imbalance of land ownership in Italy. Things were not equal, and the minority owned the majority.

The organization's vision is likened to the artist's rendering. A series of water colors of what the future home might look like. But the artist's rendering is not enough for the general contractor, subcontractors, and craftspeople to effectively and efficiently coordinate and perform their work in the construction of the home. What is needed is for the architect to translate the rendering into a detailed plan, thus eliminating or minimizing interpretation of how to go about constructing the home. That more detailed plan for the construction of the home is a set of blueprints.

The blueprint equivalent for the organizational planning team is the crafting of a strategic path and subsequent master plan. The master plan is developed by reviewing the strategies, sequencing them, specifying a timeline, and assigning accountabilities for each strategy. The specifics of doing so is discussed in just a bit.

By the leadership team specifying a strategic path and then developing a master plan prior to executing the strategy minimizes directional interpretation during the execution of the strategy. Additionally, the result of working together to develop the strategic path may cause the leadership team to revisit the vision and possibly make some modifications.

Strategy More Important Than Ever… But Needs to Be Reinvented[2]

This chapter shows you how to use the powerful vision you have crafted as a focal point for charting your strategic path. It is an example of backwards planning, where you start at the ending point (your vision) and work backward to determine how best to get there (your strategic path).

But before continuing, let's talk about the state of strategic planning in general.

Having a sound strategy, both the identity and direction dimensions, has never been more important. In this fast-paced competitive global economy, organizations need more than ever to be keenly aware of just who they are, what they stand for, what is going on in their relevant world, and how to be smart and nimble in constructively addressing current and emerging opportunities and challenges.

Today's fast-moving world is the reason that traditional strategic planning is dead. The days of developing detailed plans that look far into the future and just collect dust on bookshelves are no longer relevant. It is no longer possible to predict the future with any certainty. That is why an organization needs an approach to formulate and execute strategy that allows it to be clear about and live its core ideologies (its identity), and to continually stimulate progress in its relevant environment (its direction).

The strategic architecture described in this book meets this challenge. It allows you as the leader to *both,* define and live what you are all about, *and* be smart and nimble in addressing your current and emerging realities.

You need to continually visit and, as necessary, reinvent strategy. And it is the strategic path you chart and the resultant master plan and actions that allow you to be smart and nimble. The identity dimension (your purpose and core values), as has been stressed, is meant to be far reaching and relatively timeless. But your direction needs to be resilient to allow you to address opportunities and challenges in a timely and constructive manner.[2]

You and your leadership team need to revisit your vision, strategic path, and master plan on a regular basis to assure that your direction is what it should be. You want to critically examine your strategic assumptions and their planning implications and, as necessary, make course adjustments.

You need to see and use your strategic path as a dynamic process that needs to be continually nurtured and, as necessary, modified to be viable. This is an imperative for you and your leadership team.

View your strategic path as an ongoing strategy creation machine. When a strategy is completed, celebrate. If a strategy is no longer relevant, eliminate it. If a strategy is no longer a priority, remove it from your strategic path, perhaps to be revisited at a later date. Address emerging realities by identifying and defining new strategies and add them to your strategic path.

You and your leadership team need to have scheduled strategy meetings and periodic strategic planning sessions to keep your vision and strategic path alive and relevant. We will talk more about having these valuable get-togethers in chapter 10.

Charting Your Strategic Path[3]

What to Do

1. *Focus on the vision elements you crafted* in chapter 6 as part of your vision.

   You are going to use these vision elements to do some backwards planning. That is, you are going to identify strategic initiatives that will propel you toward the achievement of the vision elements, your desired future state.

2. *Identify one to three potential strategies for each vision element.*

3. Review the totality of the potential strategies you have identified. *Combine* strategies that naturally go together.

4. You can only effectively manage a few critical strategic imperatives at any one time. So, make sure you do not have

too much on your plate. More than a dozen is probably too many. *As necessary, delete potential strategies identified to reduce the number to a manageable level.* If you need to reduce the number of your potential strategies, *importance, urgency, and feasibility are useful criteria to use for prioritizing your list of potential strategies.*

5. Group or *synthesize similar strategies* into logical groupings. These logical groupings form *strategic themes.*

6. *Label each strategic theme* by using a carefully chosen word, or few words.

Example
Strategic Path

Shown below is the work of a planning team that, after going through the process of strategy formulation as we have discussed thus far, developed this strategic path for their non-profit organization.

Strategic Theme	Strategies
What we do	• Provide programs of interest and value to the communities we serve that will succeed and grow. • Provide creative and meaningful ideas that will help unite families, whether nuclear, multigenerational, or community. • Provide programs that are financially self-sustaining, with financial assistance provided, as needed.
Who we do it for	• Establish and market our brand or image to expand community awareness. • Build and expand the organization's family concept through outreach to any and all.

How we do it

- Establish and maintain endowment, deferred and annual giving programs, and, as needed, capital campaigns.
- Provide expanded facilities that will accommodate current and future programs. Such facilities to potentially include a pool, sports fields, multi-purpose rooms, and a gym.
- Identify and implement specific methods to ensure consistent, timely, and appropriate information flow to stakeholders, that is, staff, customers, and donors.
- Hire, develop, and encourage staff to be positive role models for the development of character.

7. *Convert your strategic path into a master plan by completing the steps below.*

First, review the example of a master plan shown below. The master plan was developed from the work the planning team did on charting the strategic path shown in the example above. They followed the steps outlined below to develop their master plan.

The master plan is an invaluable component for you and your leadership team in achieving your vision. It is your blueprint. You will use your master plan as your guiding document to implement, monitor, and, as necessary, modify your strategies as you move forward in what should be dynamic process of strategy formulation and execution.

a. *Review strategies to determine a logical sequence.* Determining sequence is critical in charting any course of action, such as constructing your master plan. *In charting a course of action, sequencing is more important than prioritizing.*

Prioritizing is important in selecting what components to include in working on a specific challenge or opportunity, such as solving a problem, making a decision, or selecting a course of action. For example, as discussed in chapter 6, selecting potential critical areas of strategic focus in conducting your situation analysis if you need to pare down the areas to focus on. Or, as just discussed above, reducing the number of potential strategies to work on. But once you have selected the components to include in whatever you are working on, you then need to logically sequence the selected components before commencing the required work to move forward.

If your strategic path contains a multitude of strategies, you may find it advantageous to first sequence your strategic themes, and then sequence the strategies within each strategic theme.

Refer to Appendix C, Interrelationship Diagram, as a useful tool to help you examine the relationships that exist amongst the various strategies. Doing so allows you to identity a logical sequence that may not be obvious.

b. *Determine start date and duration* for each strategy.

c. *Assign accountability* for each strategy. Think of the person or people accountable for each strategy as the *strategy champion*.

d. *Construct your master plan* incorporating the work you have completed as outlined in the preceding steps. Use the format as shown in the example below.

Example
Master Plan
(Developed from Strategic Path shown in previous example)

Strategic Theme	Strategy	Accountability	Timeline				
			20xx Q3Q4	20xx Q1Q2Q3Q4	20xx Q1Q2Q3Q4	20xx Q1Q2Q3Q4	20xx Q1Q2Q3Q4
What to do	• Provide programs of interest and value to the community.	Program Staff (Paul)	Ongoing				↑
		Program Committee (Judy, Bill)	Ongoing				↑
	• Provide programs that are financially self-sustaining, with financial assistance, as needed.	Program Staff Financial Staff		↑			
	• Provide creative and meaningful ideas that will help unite families, whether nuclear, multi-generational, or community.	Program Staff (Paul) Program Committee (Judy, Bill0			↑		
Who we do it for	• Establish and market our identity or image to expand community awareness.	Marketing Staff (Barbara) Marketing Committee (Len, Tom)				↑	
	• Build and expand the organization's family concept through outreach to any and all.	Marketing Staff (Director) Special Outreach Committee (Bob)					

Strategic Theme	Strategy	Accountability	Timeline				
			20xx Q3Q4	20xx Q1Q2Q3Q4	20xx Q1Q2Q3Q4	20xx Q1Q2Q3Q4	20xx Q1Q2Q3Q4
How we do it	• Establish and maintain endowment, deferred and annual giving programs, and capital campaign.	Director New Board Committee (Joe)	Ongoing (Need to be driven by both ongoing needs and strategic path) →				
	• Hire, develop, and encourage staff to be positive role models for the development of character.	Director Board Oversight	Ongoing →				
	• Identify and implement specific methods to ensure consistent, timely, and appropriate information flow to stakeholders, that is, staff, customers, and donors.	Director Marketing Staff	→				
	• Provide expanded facilities that will accommodate current and future programs. Such facilities may potentially include a pool, sports fields, multipurpose rooms, and a gym.	Task Force (Director) Board (Jane, Dick)			→		

Strategic Leadership Continues

In this chapter the necessity for you and your leadership team to be fully engaged beyond the visioning process has been stressed. You need to lead the way in charting a strategic path and a resultant master plan.

In addition, you need to stay involved in planning key actions to achieve the various strategies. This is the subject of the next chapter. This next level of blueprint is needed to ensure effective and efficient deployment of the strategy as people get to work.

9

PLANNING ACTIONS:
WHAT SPECIFICALLY ARE WE GOING TO DO?

Even if you are on the right track, you will get run over if you just sit there.

—Will Rogers

Strategies are not self-executed. Concerted time, effort, and resources are needed to make it happen.

—Author

From Architect to General Contractor

In chapter 8, *Charting a Strategic Path*, the analogy of building a custom home was likened to the strategy formulation process. In building a custom home, the architect's artist's rendering was compared to the leadership team's vision. As the architect moves from the artist rendering to a set of blueprints to provide needed specificity for the design of the home, the strategy formulation team moves from the vision to a strategic path and resultant master plan to provide needed specificity for moving forward to achieve the vision. The blueprints allow the general contractor and subcontractors to effectively and efficiently sequence, coordinate, and monitor the work of the various crafts people. The strategic path and master plan allow for the leadership team and various strategy champions to do the same with regard to the work required to achieve the vision.

Equipped with a well-crafted strategic path and properly sequenced master plan with timelines and accountabilities specified, you are now ready to move into action. As you move into action, as already discussed, roll-outs do not work. It is necessary to stay involved in the action planning and execution stages. As you move into action planning, continuing with our home building analogy, your role, and that of your leadership team, shifts from strategic architect to general contractor.

In your role as general contractor, think of yourself and your leadership team as being working leaders. You will oversee the design and implementation of the action planning process. Additionally, you may want or need to be involved in the actual performance of work depending on the size of your organization and your specific wisdom and competency relating to the work to be done as compared to others who are also going to perform the work. The decisions relative to how much you should remain solely as the working leader and how much you should "pound nails" are not to be taken lightly. You and your various strategy champions need to be deliberate relative to how best to add value to the accomplishment of the overall master plan and each strategy.

The Art of Delegating

This is the time to talk about delegating. The art of delegating is key to effectively performing the role of working leader. Below are some valuable concepts relative to the art of delegating that will be useful to you and your leadership team members as working leaders in implementing your master plan.

What Delegation Is

Delegation Entrusting responsibility and authority to others and creating accountability for desired results.

In our application, we are talking about delegating the development and implementation of plans of action for work that needs to be performed to accomplish specific strategies in your master plan.

What Delegation Is Not

Delegation is not:
- Passing the buck.
- Giving up your overall accountability.
- Refusing to make a decision by assigning it to another.
- Shirking personal responsibility.

For delegation to be truly effective, it needs to be looked upon as an investment rather than a way of getting rid of work. It also needs to be results driven rather than activity driven.

Delegating is not just passing work out. It is an opportunity to coach and develop people as well as get their inputs as you assign work. Trust and open communications are vital. When there is a lack of trust on either side, or when there is poor communication, the needed understanding and commitment is unlikely to be there.

Accountability Versus Responsibility

There is an important distinction between accountability and responsibility. And it is timely to make this distinction at this time.

Accountability The obligation to achieve *specific desired results.*

Responsibility The obligation to *complete specific work or perform specific activities.*

You can delegate responsibility; but you cannot delegate the accountability that comes with your position or role. If things do not go right relative to delegations you have made, those to whom you have delegated may be responsible, but you are still ultimately accountable.

75

Delegation Checklist

The checklist below provides for thinking through and interacting with those involved when making an important delegation. And delegating various responsibilities and authorities to achieve the specific strategies in your master plan is certainly important.

The list is comprehensive. The importance, complexity, timeline, and relevant knowledge and experience of the person or people to whom the delegation is being made should govern the thoroughness of applying these guidelines to any specific situation.

Understanding Intent and Execution

A quality conversation needs to take place when making an important delegation to assure understanding regarding the intent and the execution of the delegation.

Intent

The Situation (Context)
- What is going on?
- Why this assignment?
- Why you?
- Why now?
- What are the "givens"?
  - Scope and boundaries?
  - Commitments and limitations, for example, resources and time.
  - Who are the key stakeholders and players?

The "Whats" (The Results)
- What is the objective?
- What are the desired outcomes ("How do we know success when we see it?)

- What are the issues and concerns? (What do we need to keep our eyes on?)

Execution

Level of Authority

The levels of authority with regard to specific organizational policies, practices, or procedures can often be defined by monetary limits or ascending levels of approvals and authority. For example, capital expenditures or the hiring of professional employees. Recommendation or approval authority may be given to a lower level in the organization, with the final authority vested in a higher level in the organization.

But when it comes to the day-to-day delegation of assignments, the level of authority that comes along with that delegation needs to be discussed and understood.

The various levels possible with such delegations are outlined below.

Figure 9.1 Levels of Authority When Making Assignments

Level of Authority	Description
Investigate	Look into the situation. Gather relevant data and report back to me. I'll decide what to do.
Recommendation Authority	Look into the situation and give me your thoughts on what to do. I'll decide what to do.
Approval Authority	Examine the issue and decide what you want to do; but don't take action until you check with me and get my authorization.

| Act and Inform | Decide what you think needs to be done; do it; and let me know how it turned out. |
| Act | Take action. No need to interact with me at all. |

Assistance Needed

- Is there any special training or help needed? If so, what?
- Is there any advance communication needed with others regarding the delegation? If so:
  - Who needs to know?
  - What do they need to know?
  - How are we going to tell them?

Working Together

- How are we going to work together regarding this delegation?
- What is the frequency and the kind of interaction needed?

The frequency, type, and amount of interaction needs to be geared to the task-relevant maturity, that is competence and motivation, of the person or people to whom the delegation is being made.

The "Hows"

The work plan:
- What? (Steps)
- Who?
- When?
- Resources Needed?

Moving from the "Whats" to the "Hows"

After assuring that the "Whats" are understood, a good practice for you as a leader is to decide on the proper amount of discretion to allow for the person or people carrying out the assignment, the "Hows". As with the amount and kind of communication needed regarding the delegation as outlined above, the task-relevant maturity of the person or people to whom the assignment is being made is the primary consideration.

Think of the line between the "Whats" and the "Hows" as a dotted line, not a solid line.

On important projects you as the leader should welcome and arrange for meaningful input on the "Whats" from those who will be doing the work.

Other times, for various reasons, it may be appropriate for you as the leader to be actively engaged in the "Hows". That is, planning and implementing the actual work, including monitoring and modifying work in progress. Once again, the task-relevant maturity of the person or people performing the work will be the primary determinant.

In summary with regard to delegating important projects, initiatives, or assignments, there needs to be a quality conversation on the front end to reach a common understanding of the roles, responsibilities, and authorities of the respective parties; the desired results to be achieved (the "Whats"); and the work to be done (the "Hows").

Crafting Actions Plans

Action Plan   A process for logically defining, communicating, and implementing a course of action to effectively and efficiently complete a project.

If you don't know where you're going, you're liable
to end up somewhere else…and not even know it.

—Bob Mager

79

If you don't know where you're going, any old road will get you there.

—Will Rogers

Go Slow to Go Fast

Quality thinking and interacting at the outset of the action planning process can have huge payoffs in accomplishing the desired results. Implementation goes a lot faster and smoother with proper stakeholder understanding and commitment, and a well-crafted map by which to execute, monitor, and modify work to accomplish the desired results.

People tend to own things they help create.

—Dan Madison

Planning Time	Implementation Time

Planning Time	Implementation Time

Total Project Completion Time

Action Plans Are Scalable

The magnitude and complexity of a project dictates the appropriate amount of rigor that should go into developing the action plan.

Before identifying and describing the recommended steps in crafting an action plan, let us take a look at the idea of scalability using the context of the recommended steps as a reference.

Figure 9.2 Action Plans Are Scalable

Detail/ Complexity of Project	Appropriate Action Planning Steps				
	Project Specifications	**Implementation Considerations**	**Work Breakdown Structure**	**Work Plan**	**Team Agreements**
Minimum Level	x	x			x
Moderate Level	x	x	x	?	x
High Level	x	x	x	x	x

This chart of course serves as just a guide and not an absolute. Its purpose is just to illustrate the scalability of action plans.

Steps in Crafting an Action Plan

1. **Project specifications:** Defining success
2. **Implementation opportunities and challenges:** What lies ahead?
3. **Work breakdown structure (WBS):** Scoping out the work to be done
4. **Work plan:** Sequencing and detailing the work to be done
5. **Team agreements:** Committing to one another

Referring back to our discussion on delegating, the project specifications define the "Whats" of the project. The work breakdown structure and work plan detail the "Hows" of the project.

Now let us go through each of the steps in crafting viable action plans.

Step 1. Project Specifications: Defining Success

Defining success at the outset of any project is critical. Too often, due to a lack of awareness of the importance of specifications, not knowing how to go about defining them, and a rush to get going with the work, this crucial step is skipped, or not given the attention it deserves.

The structure for defining project specifications is shown below.

Summarize the Business Opportunity or Challenge
Why this project or initiative?
Why now?

State the Objective
Summarize in a well-stated sentence the desired end result

Define Desired Outcomes
How will we know the objective is achieved?
What does success look like?
What are evidences that success has been achieved?

Use the Goal Analysis technique described in Appendix D individually or with your leadership or planning team to define the desired outcomes.

Describe the Value
Summarize the value to the organization if the desired outcomes are achieved. To the degree possible, make it quantitative.

Summarize the Key Roles and Authorities
It makes good sense to identify and define key roles and authorities at the outset of a project, thereby minimizing issues and disputes.

Briefly define the overall project accountabilities and responsibilities, and the respective authorities. Recall the distinction made earlier between accountability and responsibility. *Accountability* being the obligation to achieve specific desired results. *Responsibility* being the obligation to complete specific work or perform specific activities. This distinction is especially important when it comes to project work.

As an example, a project manager or strategy champion may be accountable for the overall success of the project or initiative, but not personally perform a great deal of the technical work on the project.

When the project team members come from different functions, departments, or divisions, identify a *project sponsor*. The project manager can turn to the project sponsor if and when needed as issues arise that cannot be effectively resolved by the project manager. The project sponsor needs to be someone higher up in the organization who can cut across functional, departmental, and divisional boundaries on behalf of the project team to move things forward. When using a project sponsor it is important to formalize things on the front end of the project. The project specifications can serve as the *project charter*. The project sponsor *authorizes* the project. The appropriate functional and divisional heads need to *approve* the project. All parties need to sign off up front.

Timing
What are the anticipated beginning and ending dates of the project or initiative?

Example of Project Specification
Facilities Group of a nationwide organization

ACTION PLAN

Project Specifications

Business Opportunity or Challenge
A comprehensive nationwide strategy for our facility operations does not exist. Such a strategy would assure that all facilities are operated and maintained in a cost-effective manner, allowing business units to effectively and efficiently achieve their desired business units.

Objective
Develop and implement a comprehensive strategy to enhance excellence in ongoing facility operations across the nation.

Desired Outcomes
- Ongoing business unit needs are identified and met or exceeded. Such needs include lease agreements, relocations, and operational needs.
- Cost effectiveness is achieved by leveraging national contracts.
- Documented facility operational plans are used as an effective vehicle to continually identify cost efficiencies and areas for improvement. Such plans are developed and maintained in collaboration with the various business units.
- The facilities group reputation and results cause the business units to increasingly turn to us to address emerging needs and solve issues and concerns that arise.

Value
Implementation will result in increased operational efficiency and significant cost savings.

Summary of Roles and Authorities

The VP Facilities has overall accountability for the success of the project.

The Midwest Facilities Manager will serve as project manager and make proper use of corporate resources in planning and implementing the work that needs to be done to assure the success of the project.

The COO will serve as project sponsor in support of the project team.

Timing
Start: 10/202x
Complete: 4/202x

Step 2: Implementation Opportunities and Challenges

Where You Are

You have thought through what success looks like for a project by crafting the project specifications. You are now ready to plan the work that needs to be done in the form of a work breakdown structure and possibly a work plan.

The relationship between project specifications and a work breakdown structure and work plan is analogous to the relationship between your vision and your strategic path and master plan. In both cases you are defining a desired future state and then mapping out strategies or actions to achieve the success you desire. The difference is one of level in the strategy formulation process.

But before moving on to specify the work to be done to achieve project success, it is advantageous to look down the road to get a glimpse of what lies ahead. That is, implementation opportunities and challenges. Identifying potential opportunities that are present or that may emerge allows you the possibility to incorporate into your action planning process measures to help you take advantage of such opportunities that may emerge. Identifying possible challenges may allow you to incorporate preventive or contingent measures into your action planning process to help stave off or minimize potential problems that might impair the success of the project.

The three methodologies described below can facilitate your identification of possible opportunities or challenges and what to do about them.

The three methodologies are:
- Stakeholder Analysis
- Force Field Analysis
- Risk Management.

As with the entire action planning process, the rigor with which you will apply these methodologies will vary and is scalable. Your application will be governed by the importance and complexity of the project.

Stakeholder Analysis

A stakeholder is any person, group, or organization that may be directly or indirectly impacted by your project, or can directly or indirectly impact the success of the project. The number of stakeholders you may have for any particular project will of course vary. As will the potential impact for each stakeholder.

So before detailing your project plans it is important to identify the key stakeholders; the potential impact they may have on the success of your project; and, the ways to best manage these important relationships.

The key stakeholder analysis map shown below is a useful graphic for viewing key stakeholders and the potential impact they might have on your project.

Position your key stakeholders on your map according to your perception of their receptiveness toward the project and their power—position and personal—to impact it. Your perception of both of these dimensions will most likely change as you manage the relationships at the outset and during the life of the project.

Key Stakeholder Analysis Map

Example

**Project
Objective:** Refocus efforts to keep our continuous improvement efforts moving forward in the division so that we do not lose any momentum, and continue to enjoy the successful results the initiative has provided.

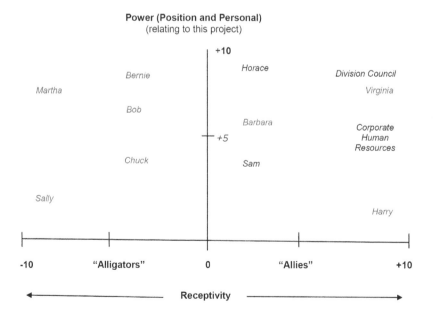

Review your Stakeholder Analysis Map and form a plan to determine: Who do we need to reach out in implementing the project? What do we need to accomplish? How are we going to reach out? Who should be involved? Also think through an appropriate strategy for ongoing communications during the course of the project.

In reaching out to your key stakeholders remember that it is unlikely that they will share the same missionary zeal you have for the project. This is natural. They may not know much about the project yet. That may a big part of why you are meeting. That is, to educate them. They may become more excited and positive once you educate them on the possible benefits to them. Maybe not. In any event, their receptivity toward the project is important to up front.

But regardless of the initial and ongoing reactions you receive, the very fact that you reached out to them and listened to their ideas, hopes, and concerns is bound to have a positive effect. You have demonstrated that you value their inputs.

You may also want to communicate what they can specifically expect from you during the course of the project. And, as applicable, what they might do to help the project be successful.

Force Field Analysis

Force Field Analysis   A tool to identify the forces that may help or hinder a change.

Change occurs when the forces make something happen are greater than the forces to keep things the same. Force Field Analysis is an excellent tool to help you identify and graph the key *driving forces* and *restraining forces* at play relative to any change or project, as well as their intensity. The input you receive from the key stakeholders you reach out to relative to your project should prove helpful in supplementing information you already are aware of regarding driving and restraining forces.

This tool is especially valuable as a reminder to identify the restraining forces as well as the driving forces at play relative to your project. Often, in one's excitement to move into action the restraining forces do not get the amount of attention they should. But such resisting forces may have a huge impact on the implementation and success of the project. You need to pay attention to ways to reduce any resistance that may be present as well as capitalizing on the benefits of the project.

In constructing a force field analysis diagram, the driving forces are put on the left of the status quo line on the diagram. The restraining forces are placed on the right side of the status quo line. The length of the arrows on each side of the diagram moving inward toward the status quo line can be used to indicate the relative strength of each of the forces identified.

The insight gained by using this tool can help you think through appropriate measures to incorporate into your action planning.

An example of a force field analysis diagram is shown on the following page

Example
Force Field Analysis

Project
Objective: Refocus efforts to keep our continuous improvement efforts moving forward in the division so that we do not lose momentum, and continue to enjoy the successful results the initiative has provided.

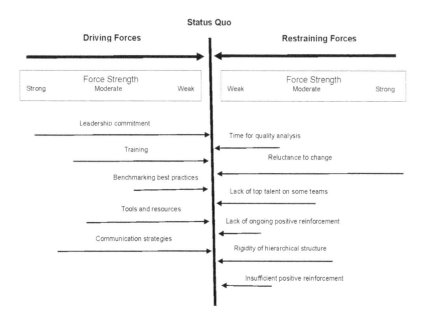

Risk Management

Use the risk management methodology to identify in advance anything that might go wrong in implementing your project, and what preventive or contingent actions you might take to counteract such possibilities.

For example, when thinking of fire prevention when constructing a building, a preventive action would be to use concrete instead of wood. An example of a contingent action would be to install a fire sprinkler system.

What to Do

1. Review your project specifications and identify any potential problems.

2. Assess the probability and seriousness of each potential problem.

3. Develop any appropriate *preventive actions.*

4. Develop any appropriate *contingent actions.* That is, actions to take if and when the potential problem occurs.

   Identify a trigger for each contingent action. A trigger being an indicator that will cause you to initiate timely action to deal with the problem. In addition, you may find it wise to designate a point person for each contingent action.

5. As applicable, embed appropriate steps or measures into your work plan to specify preventive or contingent actions.

Step 3. Work Breakdown Structure (WBS): Scoping Out the Work to be Done

Where You Are

- You have well-articulated project specifications that are understood and accepted by your key stakeholders.

- You have identified and analyzed implementation opportunities and challenges. You will implement appropriate actions to take advantage of identified opportunities and constructively address identified challenges. You may see fit to incorporate some of these actions into your specific plans as you move forward.

As previously discussed, action plans need to be scalable. You will take into account the complexity and detail needed in determining whether to use both a WBS and a resultant work plan. Or just a WBS. Or you may decide that neither is needed.

The amount of rigor you decide you need in planning the implementation of a specific strategic imperative you have identified is not necessarily related to its importance. For example, a leadership team may think that the project specifications they have defined and the implementation opportunities and challenges they have identified may suffice, and that there is no need to scope out the work (WBS) or craft a resultant detailed work plan. The leadership team may just see the need for them to commit to specific actions and behaviors for the foreseeable future to accomplish a strategy. They will wait for appropriate opportunities to arise before springing into action. But they will want to develop implementation team agreements, as described in step 5. In the team agreements they will detail their specific commitments to one another as well as how they are going to hold each accountable for living up to those commitments.

Work Breakdown Structure (WBS)	A methodology for identifying and grouping the various work packages and related tasks for each work package.
	The WBS can serve on its own as an implementation plan, Or, if greater specificity is needed, the WBS can serve as a useful map or outline for crafting a detailed work plan.

The WBS is a valuable tool. It can stand on its own as an action planning tool, serving as a punch list of tasks to be performed. Or, it can serve as a transitional methodology between your project specifications and a detailed work plan.

The number of levels of breakdown should fit the size and complexity of the project. For most projects three levels of breakdown are sufficient. The three levels would be the project objective, the work packages, and the tasks or activities to be performed for each work package.

What to Do

1. Write down your project objective.

2. Use the Affinity Diagram described in Appendix A as a useful tool to identify the logical groupings of work that need to be performed to accomplish the project objective. These are your work packages.

3. Identify and list under each work package the tasks that need to be performed in that work package.

Example
Work Breakdown Structure (WBS)

Project Objective: Identify strategies to reduce the total costs of general employee training at the operations facility while maintaining the required safety and quality standards and without unduly sacrificing quality of the overall training program.

Project Formulation	Getting Started	Data Gathering and Analysis	Recommendations
• Craft Project • Craft Project Charter and obtain authorization • Identify implementation opportunities and challenges	• Select project team • Have initial meeting • Craft team agreements and accountabilities and get buy-in	• Develop "Future State" • Develop "Current State" • Develop strategies to close the gap	• Craft recommendations to implement strategies Specifications • Present recommendations • Obtain authorization to develop a project plan to move forward

In this example, the project objective is the first order of breakdown. The work packages are the second order of breakdown. And the bulleted items under each work package represent the tasks to be performed in that work package.

If a work plan is called for, sequence the work packages. If needed, use the Interrelationships Digraph described In Appendix C to help you do so.

4. Work Plan: Sequencing and Detailing the Work to be Done

Where You Are

- You have well-articulated project specifications that are understood and accepted by your key stakeholders.

- You have identified and analyzed implementation opportunities and challenges. You will implement appropriate actions to take advantage of identified opportunities and constructively address identified challenges. You may see fit to incorporate some of actions into your specific plans as you move forward.

- You have used a WBS to scope out the project work that needs to be done.

- You have decided that given the complexity and detail of the project it is appropriate to craft work plan.

Work Plan	A methodology for sequencing and detailing the specific work to be done and related accountabilities, timing, and resources needed, to complete the work to achieve the project objective.

The work plan format described below works well for most projects. If the complexity of a project warrants, software programs, such as Microsoft Project, are available to provide additional rigor. Such software programs allow for greater scheduling detail, resource allocation, cost planning, project tracking, and reporting progress.

There are also additional project planning methodologies available such as Critical Path Method (CPM) and Program Evaluation and Review Technique (PERT) for large complex projects. Organizations whose lifeblood is project management most often have dedicated staff or use consultants to formulate such detailed project plans.

Work Plan Format

The work plan format described is comprised of three components: Program, Schedule, and Resource Allocation. Each of these components is described below.

Program

Steps	Accountability
The sequence necessary to effectively and efficiently work the plan. If called for by the rigor of the project, the steps can be arranged in phases. Also, as needed, important notations pertaining to specific steps can be summarized under a "Detail" caption for that step.	The person or people accountable for ensuring that a specific step is effectively and efficiently achieved.

Schedule

The anticipated beginning and ending dates for each step.

Resource Allocation

An estimate of the resources needed, as applicable to complete each step.

People-Days	Financial	Space & Equipment	Information
People-days required to complete the specific step.	Out-of-pocket costs, if any, for the step.	Special space and equipment needs, if any, to complete the step. Often, if there are any special space and equipment needs, the requirement will span several steps, or the project as a whole.	Data or information needed, if any, to complete the specific step.

The suggested structure for a complete action plan, including the work plan, is shown on the following two pages.

Action Plan

Project Specifications

**Business Opportunity
or Challenge:**

Objective:

**Desired
Outcomes:**

Value:

**Key Roles and
Authorities:**

Timing:
Start:
Completion:

Work Plan

Program		Schedule		Resource Allocation			
Steps	Acct	Begin	End	People—Days	Financial	Space & Equipment	Information

Project Control

Just as the complexity of the project should dictate the rigor of the project planning process, the control methods used to monitor and modify work in progress should also align with the magnitude and complexity of the work plan. The work plan outlined above has proven to be sufficient as a focus for most projects to monitor progress.

You as the leader, strategy champion, or project manager will want to have regular progress review meetings. You may also want to establish progress checkpoints, perhaps pegged to project milestones or key dates. If applicable, you may want to specify quantitative measures to help monitor progress.

Step 5: Team Agreements

Regardless of the project planning rigor needed for your project, you will want to create agreements with the key team players or, as applicable, the entire team relative to the necessary *commitments* that need to be made to one another to ensure project success. You will also want to determine the *mutual accountabilities* that need to be followed to assure that such commitments are honored.

Team Agreements	Principles and ideas the leader and team members deem essential to allow them to effectively work together and to manage the work to be done.

Creating team agreements is an important activity that helps the team leader ensure that the team is working productively together. *Team agreements are applicable to ongoing teams, such as leadership teams, as well as time-limited teams, such as project teams.*

Team agreements are analogous to core values. Both need to be few in number and critical to success. The distinctions are that whereas core values are essential and enduring beliefs to guide everyday thinking and behavior of the organization as a whole; team agreements are commitments the leader and team member make to one another regarding principles and ideas they hold to be important in managing team member relationships and the wok of the team.

In his best-selling book, *Principles*[1], Ray Dalio, founder of Bridgewater, a large hedge fund organization, espouses the importance of principles to live and work by. His message to leaders is that they need to operate by principles that are so clearly laid out that their logic can easily be assessed by the leader and others to determine if they are walking the talk.

Listed below are three questions recommended by Allan McCarthy that are helpful in creating team agreements.[2]

In creating team agreements with your team, consider these three questions:

1. Think of the *characteristics of great teams* that you know of, or been a part of. List those characteristics that promoted success.

2. Given your knowledge and experience with successful teams, and your knowledge of this team, what are *the key agreements you think are most important for this team to manage its team dynamics*?

3. How should the team members go about *holding each other accountable for each agreement*? If the team or team member is not following the agreement, how is the situation constructively handled?

Below are a few samplings of some team agreements from various teams. These are meant to be samplings only, and not meant to be copied. While it is not necessarily a bad thing to borrow other's thoughts on formulating team agreements, any adapting must be taken with careful thought to assure that the agreements are consistent with the voice and convictions of the team leader and team members, and the work of the team.

- Create a safe place where team members can express divergent points of view openly and passionately without fear of being ridiculed. Constructive conflict needs to be encouraged, not discouraged. Doing so allows for better decision making and understanding. *Accountability: Speak up if and when you feel invalidated. We need to clear up such situations when they occur. Also, we need to periodically discuss just how rigorous our transparency is.*

- Have growth mindsets, not fixed mindsets. Need to be willing and able to change our mental models based upon new knowledge and experiences. *Accountability: Question each other when we sense someone is being mired in a fixed mindset. Why are they thinking that way?*

- Come to team meetings prepared to discuss any items on the agenda, what is going on with regard to your project responsibilities, and any action items you have been assigned in previous meetings. *Accountability: Call each other out on "ball dropping" without getting emotional and accusatory.*

- At the end of each team meeting, agree on conclusions, actions to be taken, and what is to be and not to be communicated outside the meeting, as well as the timing and individual responsibilities regarding such communication. *Accountability: Start each meeting with feedback regarding agreed-to conclusions, actions to be taken, and related communications.*

Listed below are the agreements Ray Dalio found to be most important in working with his teams:[3]

1. Put our honest thoughts on the table.
2. Have thoughtful disagreements in which people are willing to shift their opinions as they learn.
3. Have agreed-upon ways of deciding, for example, voting, having clear authorities, if disagreements remain so that we can move beyond them without resentments.

These samplings should provide you with a good understanding of what team agreements are, their importance, and how powerful they can be.

This concludes our discussion of strategy formulation. The intent was to give you the requisite clarity, confidence, and competence to engage in quality thinking and interacting with your leadership team to create and sustain a sound strategy.

We now move to executing the strategy. Making it all happen.

III

EXECUTING STRATEGY

....

Parts I and II are all about how to go about developing and updating a sound strategy.

In the final part of the book, we turn to how to go about executing your sound strategy. And this is where many organizations fall down. They may have a sound strategy, but for whatever reason they do not execute it well. It may be the press of business, or lack of genuine commitment, or a host of other reasons. The net upshot is that not only does the strategy not get implemented as it should, but doubts may be created related to the importance and efficacy of the strategic planning process.

In chapter 10 we discuss the essential leadership behaviors, important concepts and practices, and helpful operational mechanisms to make it all happen in working the strategy.

10

ENABLING THE ORGANIZATION: WORKING THE STRATEGY

Perhaps the most promising trend in our thinking about leadership is the growing conviction that the purposes of the group are best served when the leader helps followers to develop their own initiative, strengthens them in the use of their own judgment, enables them to grow and to become better contributors.

—John W. Gardner

People need models, not critics.

—John Wooden

Enabling the Organization

• Essential Leadership Behaviors
• Important Concepts and Practices
• Helpful Operational Mechanisms

Strategy Execution

Regardless of how well you as the leader and your leadership team have done in formulating a sound strategy (both identity and direction) you need to stay genuinely involved in executing the strategy if it is to effectively and efficiently implemented. You do not want to make the same mistake that so many leaders and leadership teams make in thinking that their work is done after formulating strategy and just "rolling it out". You and your leadership team need to lead in executing the strategy.

Let us discuss the leadership behaviors, concepts, and practices, and some helpful operational mechanisms that can make for successful execution of your strategy.

Communicating the Strategy

You and your leadership team need to plan, coordinate and implement your communications regarding your strategy or changes or changes in your strategy to assure understanding and to gain commitment. You will want to use a variety of communication methods in delivering your key messages consistently and frequently.

It is important to communicate not only the elements of the strategy but also the rationale driving the strategy, be it the identity or direction dimension. Depth is also important. Without depth, clarity is sterile and inspiration is inadequate. And above all else, you need to be authentic.[1]

In structuring your important messages, you want to make use of the important communication channels we discussed earlier in chapter 3, *Clarifying Your Values"*. These three values are important to executing your strategy as well as living your values. To repeat, the three channels are: the *factual channel* (the words or content of the message; speaking from the head); the *emotional channel* (feelings of both the speaker and the listeners; speaking from the heart); and, the *symbolic channel* (stories, examples, and metaphors).[2]

Ron Crossland points out that contemporary research has disproved the idea that the brain works as a computer, storing different kinds of information in different areas of the brain. Rather, people look for sense and meaning by combining or recombining information from a vast network of systems in the brain. Therefore, the leader needs to think of communicating important messages like making a movie. That is, the leader needs to convey information using all three channels to help the listeners fill in the blanks from their own mental sources.[3]

As also previously mentioned, the work of Chip Heath and Dan Heath supports the importance of the three communication channels. In addition, the Heath brothers give us some sound recommendations to make ideas stick when using the factual channel.[4]

Specifically, *in using the factual channel* when communicating your important messages, to gain traction your ideas need to be:[4]

Simple	What is the *intent* of your idea? As soon as people know the intent, they begin generating their own solutions. What is the *core of your idea?*
Unexpected	The first problem of communications is getting people's attention. And the most basic way to get people's attention is to break the pattern. You need to open gaps before you close them. *"Start a fire, and then build a bridge."*
Concrete	Concreteness creates a shared turf on which people can collaborate. Being concrete is not difficult, and it does not require a lot of effort. The barrier is simply that we often don't realize when we slip into abstract speaking.
Credible	Honesty and trustworthiness are paramount. Details, statistics, and examples make ideas more credible.

*Let's talk a bit about the critical leadership characteristic—**credibility**.* This is important. Credibility is how leaders earn the trust and confidence of their constituents.[5]

The results discovered by Jim Kouzes and Barry Posner regarding the *characteristics of admired leaders* have been consistent over decades, around the globe, and across all organizational sectors. This is important in that it is these admired characteristics that go into establishing a leader's credibility.[6]

According to their research, the majority of people look for and admire leaders who are *honest, forward-looking, inspiring,* and *competent.* These four characteristics consistently top the list of characteristics of admired leaders.

In their research, *honesty* consistently ranks as number one. In conversations I have had with Jim Kouzes as to where *integrity* ("walking the talk") fits in. His answer is that it is included in their definition of honesty.

Regarding *forward-looking.* This of course is the quality this book is attempting to help the leader develop by providing the clarity, confidence, and competence to do so.

Regarding *inspiring.* Inspiring does not mean that the leader needs to be the "rah-rah" type. But it does mean that the leader needs to work on being dynamic, uplifting, enthusiastic, positive, and optimistic.

Regarding *competency.* Competency refers to the leader being knowledgeable and skillful in all three types of organizational work as discussed in chapter 1—leadership, management work, and technical work. And do not fall into the trap of thinking, as many leaders do. That is the false premise that the leader needs to be all-knowing and all-wise. In fact, in his research, Jim Collins discovered quite the opposite. He found that *truly effective leaders build greatness through a paradoxical blend of **personal humility** and **professional will*** (emphasis added). Collins states that great leaders are a study in duality: modest and willful. And humble and fearless.[7]

In using the *emotional channel* do not shy away from being *genuinely transparent*. Speak from the heart in being open and honest about your hopes and concerns. *Vulnerability* builds trust. In being vulnerable you are liberating yourself from your ego to speak genuinely.

Berne Brown has a lot to say about *vulnerability*.[8]

- Vulnerability is not a weakness. In fact, it is just the opposite.
- People have typically shied away from vulnerability because of the fear of being ashamed.
- Vulnerability needs to be embraced and developed.
- Vulnerability is the pathway to courage. You can't have courage without vulnerability.
- We are talking relationship vulnerability; not systemic vulnerability, for example, "I am incompetent". "I am no good".
- True leadership is not about pretending to have the right answers; but rather to stay curious and ask the right questions.
- True leadership is not about avoiding difficult conversations and situations, but rather being vulnerable when it is necessary to do good work.
- The courage to be vulnerable is to show up when you can't predict or control the outcome. Not winning or losing. Willingness to be seen and heard.
- The skills to be developed include empathy, connection, and the courage to start.

Let's call a time out here. What research tells us about leadership credibility, the characteristics of admired leaders, the qualities of leadership greatness, and vulnerability calls for a pause in the action. What has just been discussed is too important to just gloss over. It calls for reflection.

So before moving on, reflect on how these characteristics, attributes, of qualities relate to you personally as a leader. To what extent do you agree or disagree with these findings and recommendations? If you disagree with any of these findings and recommendations, just what is it that you disagree with? If you find quite a bit of wisdom in these findings and recommendations, to what extent does your current leadership behavior reflect these findings and recommendations? Are there any changes you would like to make in your current leadership behavior based upon these findings and recommendations? If so, what are they?

As we all are well aware, making personal behavioral change is not so easy. So, if you want to make any changes to your current leadership behavior please spend some time with *Appendix E, "Self-Coaching"*. You will find a practical and proven methodology to help you make whatever change you are thinking of making.

Another important consideration for you to be aware of in structuring your messages is that *people have subconscious priorities and behavioral preferences that affect how they take in information and what they deem important.* Being aware of these tendencies can help you better pace with those you are attempting to communicate with, individually or as a group.

So, let's discuss these subconscious priorities and behavioral preferences.

Representational System

Most people have a preference in how they use the three senses of seeing, hearing, and feeling to take in (receive) and transmit information (send). We all use all three senses, but most people have a preference. And to some people this preference is quite pronounced. The other two senses, smelling and tasting, do not play much of a role in communications unless those senses are called for to assess a task at hand, such as tasting a food item. Bandler and Grinder called this preference for favoring one of the three senses the *representational system*. They referred to the three senses as *visual* (seeing), *auditory* (hearing), and *kinesthetic* (feeling; experiencing things).[9]

With people you interact with on a frequent basis you should be able to pick out these preferences if indeed they do exist. Tune into the kinds of words people use on a consistent basis.

For example:

- *"I see your point."*
  "But that is only my view."
  (Visual)

- *"Sounds good to me."*
  "At least that's what I hear."
  (Auditory)

- *"I think I have a good feel for what you are trying to say."*
  "My experience has always been that…"
  (Kinesthetic)

In serious conversation, the value of knowing one's preferred representational system allows you to align with your receiver's preferred system when speaking to enhance rapport and gain clarity.

When speaking to a group on important matters, such as your strategy, you want to attempt to incorporate all three preferences that make up the representational system. That is, visual, auditory, and kinesthetic. You can do so by perhaps reinforcing the words with handouts, using visual aids, and involving your audience by having them do something.

Behavioral Preferences

In like manner, most people have preferred natural thinking and behavioral preferences or styles, or a blending of such preferences or styles. And because they are a natural part of a person, most often such preferences occur at a subconscious level.

There are many models and related assessment instruments that focus on such natural thinking and behavioral tendencies. I am going to use the popular *DISC* model to help you understand the nature of these preferences and why such understanding can be important to you in pacing with others in trying to achieve understanding of your message.

The four *DISC* behavioral styles are described below:

Behavioral Style Description/Preferences

D	Dominance	Driver; results; assertive; action; bottom line; control; independence; decisive.
I	Influencing	Relationships; people; persuasive; seeks approval; dislikes structure.
S	Steadiness	Progress; collaboration; stability; teamwork; harmony; staying the course.
C	Conscientiousness	Security; stability; proven; thorough; facts; assurance; patient; standards.

Although I am not promoting the DISC model or any of its related assessment instrumentation, it is good at what it does for general audiences.[10] There are other types of assessments for specific different purposes and audiences. For example, leadership, organizational, sales, learning, and emotional intelligence assessments.

Although *DISC* or similar models can be very useful, such frameworks are not mandatory to better understand the thinking and behavioral preferences of people you interact with on a frequent basis. Just pay attention.

The value once again of identifying such preferences is that in important conversations you can gain greater rapport and be more effective by, no matter what your own natural thinking and behavioral preferences are, *adapting to the thinking and behavioral preferences* of whomever you are interacting with. Think of yourself as a rubber band stretching out to meet the person you are interacting with.

And *when speaking to a group* about important matters such as strategic initiatives or related projects, you want to incorporate thinking and behavioral preferences into your communications. For example, stressing the importance of results for the D types; the importance of improved relationships for the I types; the importance of steady progress and collaboration for the S types; and, the importance of the facts and the proven for the S types.

Coaching

Implementing your strategy provides you a tremendous opportunity to coach leaders and strategy champions in your organization. One focus of coaching could be to help leaders translate the overall organizational direction and its execution for application to their respective organizational areas of responsibility. The goal in so doing is to align and support their functional, departmental, of division responsibilities with that of the organization as a whole. Another area of potential coaching focus could be to help them develop practices they can engage in to model the way for their people.

Making Performance Matter

Through both your formal and informal reward and recognition practices you need to make performance matter for you leaders and their respective organizational units in executing the strategy.

> Catch people doing things right and let them know about it… in no uncertain terms.
>
> —Bob Mager

Integrating Strategy into the Budgeting Process

You need to ensure that your strategic initiatives are properly funded. To do so you may need to make sure that they are appropriately included and accounted for in your organization's budgeting process. Some strategic initiatives may go beyond a specific budgeting year or years in your budgeting process.

Strategy Meetings

In working your strategy, it is critical that you develop the discipline and structure to devote quality thinking and interacting with your leadership team focusing solely on the strategy.

Meetings are the primary medium you have to interact with your leadership team. But, as you undoubtedly know many, if not most, meetings are ineffective and inefficient. Many may not be necessary.

Patrick Lencioni states that are two primary reasons for bad meetings. The first is that most are just plain boring. The second is that they lack contextual structure.[11]

Lack of Contextual Structure

Let's talk about the second cause of bad meetings first. That is, a lack of contextual structure.

Lencioni likens the lack of contextual structure to what he calls "meeting stew". That is, trying to fit all business into one meeting rather than separating things into different meetings for different purposes.[12]

Having meetings dedicated to working your strategy is critical to effectively executing the strategy. You need to devote quality time to monitoring and possibly modifying your strategy, rather than sandwiching such important deliberations into other operational or tactical meetings you may have.

The three types of strategy meetings described below are for your consideration.

Periodic Strategy Meetings.

No less than quarterly, perhaps monthly, lasting from two to four hours. Your leadership team, strategy champions, and perhaps key contributors attend.

The purpose is to review overall progress on strategic initiatives in your master plan. And, as necessary, make course adjustments. Also, to dig into critical issues. And as needed to add or delete strategic initiatives in your master plan. Your strategy machine in action. Strategic initiatives which seemed important may, for whatever reason, no longer be so. They can be deferred or eliminated. Emerging opportunities or challenges may be deserving of crafting a new strategic initiative.

Ad Hoc Strategy Meetings.

As needed. Bringing key players together regarding a specific strategic initiative or initiatives to discuss issues or concerns that need immediate attention.

Annual Planning and Review Meetings

One to two days involving your leadership team and perhaps some other key contributors.

Reviewing your organization's identity, that is, purpose and core values, to assure that everything is still relevant. Discussing how we are living our core values.

Reviewing and updating the master plan by conducting a current situation analysis, and crafting an updated interim vision and resultant strategic path and master plan.

Boring Meetings

Boredom should not be an issue in your strategy meetings because those attending your strategy meetings, that is, your leadership team members, specific strategy initiative champions, and perhaps key contributors, are committed because they have "skin in the game". They are accountable for a specific strategic initiative or have specific responsibilities. They have a stake in the meeting.

Lencioni suggests that to enliven meetings they should be more like a movie.[14] A movie that grabs your attention has conflict, which is the heart of drama. It often also is unpredictable, and gets you to thinking and wondering. [13]

Below are some important concepts for you to seriously think about in conducting your meetings. They can counter boredom in your strategy meetings, or any meeting you sponsor. Plus, these ideas make for more productive meetings.

- In your meetings you want to encourage, not avoid, conflict. That is, the right kind of conflict. *Constructive conflict.* Constructive conflict is *task conflict* as opposed to *relationship conflict.* Task conflict is about problem solving, decision making, and charting a course of action. Relationship conflict has to do with individuals not respecting of caring for one another, for whatever reason. You as a leader want to optimize task conflict in discussing important matters. And you want to minimize relationship conflict.

  To encourage constructive conflict, you need to develop a team culture that encourages people to express their divergent points of view without having the fear of being invalidated or embarrassed. You need to provide psychological safety. You might consider crafting one of your team agreements and corresponding accountability to have the team commit to this important concept. We discussed team agreements in chapter 9. You need to create a Circle of Safety and Support within which team members can speak freely without fear of reprisal.[14]

  Such a Circle of Safety and Support will only work if you as the leader make it work. You do so by developing the necessary trust within the team by modeling the way;

assuring that team members treat each another with respect and dignity; and, that everyone continually strives to seek to understand one another, and be understood. The goal being to understand and accept one another's point of view. Not to necessarily agree.

Principle of Reciprocity	If I take the time and make a genuine effort to truly understand your meaning, feeling, or motive on an important matter to you, to me, or both of us, you may feel a little indebted and do the same for me when it becomes my turn to talk.

—William H. Pemberton

- "Mine" for potential areas of disagreement in advance so that important issues and challenges that can best be resolved through healthy dialogue are included in your meeting.

- In your meetings focus on the current and the future, not the past. "What is going on?" and "What are we going to do about it?" If necessary, participants can review past information and data in advance to properly prepared for the meeting.

- If appropriate, rotate team meeting roles periodically.

- As appropriate, periodically have team members make presentations to the team.

- Periodically schedule people to address the team who might have something germane to say that would be of interest to the team.

- Assign a team member to be the meeting scribe. The role is not to "take minutes". Rather, the role is to: a) make note of any important conclusions or decisions made and actions to be taken during the course of the meeting; and, b) to at the end of the meeting read any such notations back to the team to assure there is understanding as to the conclusions and decisions made and any action items. Action items are to include who is accountable and the timing.

Also, at the end of each meeting discuss any communications that should, or not occur, outside of the meeting. Include accountabilities, timing, and communication specifics.

- At the front end of each meeting begin by having any individuals accountable for action items from previous meetings give a progress report.

Cascading the Strategy

Once the strategy for the organization as a whole is operational, the next step is to equip the various organizational levels to formulate and execute their own strategies that align with and support the overall strategy. The size of the organization will of course dictate the complexity of the cascade for any given organization.

The ideal is that the formulation and execution of a sound strategy such as that described in this book starts at the top and then effectively cascades down through the organization. But in organizations where such a process does not exist, enlightened leaders at any level in an organization can use the Strategic Framework described in the book to develop a sound strategy for their specific organizational unit.

Allan McCarthy identifies three broad organizational levels that are typically involved in cascading strategy in larger organizations.[15]

Figure 10.1: Organizational Levels in Cascading Strategy

Organizational Level

Strategic	Top level strategy formulation and execution.
Cross-functional	Aligning efforts across the organization in support of the overall organizational strategy. "Flying in formation." A deep understanding of the overall organizational strategy begins to be embedded in the organization.
Functional	The respective functions, departments, and divisions develop their respective strategies that align with and support the strategic direction from above. Cross-functional organization level needs to work through a complete planning cycle before cascading to the functional level. Functional expertise needs to be involved.

As the overall organizational strategy is cascaded across and down through the organization, the comprehensiveness at the lower levels does not need to be as thorough. *Regarding the identity dimension*, every organization unit should establish its unique purpose. The overall organizational core values themselves may be appropriate throughout the organization, or perhaps slightly modified. But the operational definitions need to be customized to fit the realities of the specific organizational units. *Regarding the direction dimension*, any big dreams that exist probably do not need to be formalized; but a translatable vision and the resultant strategic path, master plan, and actions need to be formulated. And at the lowest functional levels of the organization, there should be a goal setting process that aligns with and supports the direction from above.

Assessing Strategic Impact

You assess progress toward your vision by monitoring and modifying work in progress relative to your various strategic initiatives. You do so by, as previously discussed, having regular productive strategy meetings, and by having checkpoints and perhaps specific measures embedded in the projects crafted to achieve the various strategic initiatives.

But the reason you formulate and execute a strategic direction is not just to achieve strategic initiatives. Achieving them is great, but what you are really interested in is their impact on overall organizational performance.

So, let's discuss ways to go about monitoring overall organizational performance. And in so doing, be in a place to assess the impact that your strategic direction is having on the performance.

There are basically two types of management control you have as a leader: *management by inspection*, or personal inspection, and *management by exception*, or making use of performance measures. Each type of control has its advantages and disadvantages. Let's talk about each.

Management by Inspection

This type of management control is popularly referred to as "management by walking around" (MBWA). Getting out and seeing what is going on for yourself.

The advantage of this type of control is that you can get a visceral feel for what is going on by personally observing performance in specific areas of your choosing. It also provides a tremendous opportunity for you to engage with people. In so doing you can receive constructive feedback and get ideas for improvement. It also provides you an opportunity to emphasize what you think is important, provide constructive feedback or your own, and to voice appreciation and encouragement.

The disadvantage is that it takes time, and you may not be able to get the true picture. Also, if you are not genuine and do not handle such visitations effectively, your presence could evoke unintended fear as you make your rounds. That is unless you want to inject some fear.

For the above reasons, the term *"Caring by Walking Around"* (CBWA)[16] is recommended.

CBWA is really a matter of attitude. In CBWA you are authentic in your travels to see what is going on, and not out to just snoop around. And if you are genuine and caring, do not think that your presence is not appreciated. By your presence, you are telling people that they are important. You care about what they are doing and what they have to say. And again, CBWA allows you to emphasize what you think is important. Also, as needed, to provide some rationale regarding some of the organizational strategies and activities that impact them.

As the old management adage goes: "What the boss inspects, the boss expects".

Management by Exception

Management by exception entails developing specific performance measures and monitoring progress by assessing actual performance results against those measures.

The advantage of relevant performance measures is that you get feedback on an ongoing basis that helps you assess performance results and identify trends. Such measures can be of help in gauging success and identifying potential performance issues and concerns in a timely manner. Performance measures can also help you identify possible areas of critical strategic focus when conducting a situation analysis as part of the strategy formulation process.

The disadvantage is that you cannot measure everything quantitatively. The performance you can measure quantitively will be largely dependent on the nature of your business. Sometimes surveys or focus groups may be appropriate to use in lieu of quantitative performance measures.

Establishing meaningful performance measures involves these critical steps:

1. *Identify the Critical Success Factors (CSFs) for your organization.*

   The CSFs are the critical few things that are vital to the success of your organization. Things that can make or break you.

   Do not make the mistake of creating measures just because something is easy to measure. Doing so can create a misallocation of management and staff focus and resultant inefficient use of time and resources.

2. Review your CSFs and determine if and how each can be measured. Ask the following questions:

   • Can this CSF be measured quantitively?

     If yes,:
     ▪ Describe the appropriate measure or measures.
     ▪ Prescribe the specific formula or formulas to be used to gather the necessary data.

- Determine just how the data is going to be collected? What? When? Who?

If no:
- What alternative means can be used to assess results for this CSF?
  Surveys? Focus groups?
- And, of course, CBWA.
- Is there any advantage in formalizing any CBWA activities?

Clarify Terminology

Clearly define the terms you will be using in establishing and monitoring the performance measures you will be using. Assure that they are understood and applied properly.

The following terminology and definitions are recommended:

Measure	Brief description of the performance measure and its quantitative formulation. The quantitative formulation is the description or formula explaining how the specific number for the measure is to be computed.
Target	A realistic quantitative standard you are shooting for on an ongoing basis for a specific measure. Realistic being defined as challenging, but doable. It could be a specific number, dollar amount, percentage, or survey results. Whatever would represent success when you see it. Obtaining and sustaining performance that is on target represents success.
Actual	The result for a specific measure for the time period being measured.
Variance	The difference between the target and the actual for a specific period of time.
Goal	A desired performance that is set for a given time period that varies from the target.

These terms and definitions seem straightforward, and they are. But they are included here because they are often ill-defined and misapplied, leading to confusion, frustration, and poor management.

Let's discuss a bit.

When you first identify a measure, most often a realistic target cannot be set because you do not yet have enough history or data to establish a firm target. If so, set a temporary target just to get started. You can adjust it later once you have enough experience collecting data for the specific measure.

When you have set a target you think is challenging, yet realistic, and represents success, treat it as being a firm target. Obviously, you should change the target if circumstances affecting the target change substantially. For example, the introduction of new, additional, or improved technology. Or added or reduced staffing.

Do not, and this is important, change the target just because you reached it. Doing so defeats the purpose of having the target. Instead, if there is a substantial variance between the target and the actual, and it is not an "outlier" occurrence, set a goal to move toward the target. Conversely, if for some reason you want to put effort forward to exceed the target, and succeed, do not change the target just because you exceeded it. When you constantly change a target just because you reached it or exceed it, you end up chasing down perfection. And you are likely to experience the law of diminishing returns. That is, the more time and resources you pour into a specific measure trying to achieve perfection has a tipping point. The tipping point being that the value gained by applying additional resources does not outweigh the time and cost of the additional resources. In other words, it is not a wise investment. It also can become extremely frustrating to the managers and people performing the work.

Balanced Scorecard

If the nature of your organizational business lends itself to establishing a multitude or performance measures, and you deem it worthwhile to collect and analyze the data on an ongoing basis, aim to develop what is popularly referred to as a *balanced scorecard*.

The balanced scorecard concept was pioneered by Robert Kaplan and David Norton[17]. Its purpose is to develop a comprehensive performance management system rather than fixating on just a few measures. And, it is argued, in the case of assessing the performance of the organization as a whole, such measures are often financial. And, as the argument goes, concentrating solely or primarily on financial measures leads to an overemphasis on short-term, bottom-line results. This myopic focus then leads to an obsession with tactical thinking and behavior, rather than a balance of tactical and strategic leadership thinking and behavior. The overall strength and health of the organization suffers as a result.

The four perspectives, as the authors call them, organizations should consider in developing a balanced scorecard are: financial, customer, process, and learning and growth. The first two of these are external perspectives, and the last two being internal perspectives.

Shown below are some examples of some typical measures that for the various perspectives.

Figure 10.2: Examples of Typical Measures in a Balanced Scorecard

Perspective	Measure
Financial	• Revenue growth • Margins • Expense management
Customer	• New customers • Customer retention • Customer satisfaction
Process	• New product development • E-commerce capability • Process improvement
Learning and Growth	• Employee development • Employee satisfaction • Turnover

Some organizations use the practice of color coding the variances on their reports to highlight the current status. For example, using traffic lights, green light = going well; yellow light = "heads up"; red light = needs attention.

If you think establishing a balanced scorecard makes sense for your organization, be it the organization as a whole or an organizational unit, approach it slowly. Do some experimentation. Develop your own framework perspectives if you want. And, of course, customize your measures. And remember to incorporate the important critical success factor (CSFs) concept when thinking of potential performance measures. And, to repeat a forementioned caveat, do not include performance measures in your balanced scorecard design just because they are easy to measure. They need to represent CSFs.

Assessing Yourself as Strategy Leader

Let's now turn from assessing the performance of the organization to assessing your own performance as the strategic leader.

The invaluable point to be made here is that in making the shift in focus from measuring organizational success to measuring your own success as strategy leader is to use a completely different mindset. When assessing your own performance, rather than looking forward and measuring progress toward the achievement of the vision, both interim and big dream, assess your performance by measuring backwards. Specific things you have accomplished in your leadership role. By *measuring gains and not gaps.*

This simple but profound concept comes from the work of Dan Sullivan.[18] Dan is a strategy coach who has worked with thousands of entrepreneurs spanning decades. In struggling with the enigma of why the vast majority of these high achievers were so consistently unhappy he came to the conclusion that the root cause is how they measured their success. When measuring against their ideals, whatever they might be, they consistently came up short. The reasons are that the ideals were distant, ever changing, often not measurable, many times not attainable. In addition, they often did not have sufficient control of the outcomes.

The perception of success of these high achievers made a drastic shift when he got them to measure their success backwards. To focus on gains instead of gaps. To focus on strides they had made on their respective personal journeys, the gains, instead of focusing on the distance they still had to travel to achieve their respective ideals, the gaps.

This shift in mindset is definitely germane to use as a strategy leader. The causes for these entrepreneurs' discontent are some of the same issues you as a strategy leader have in assessing your leadership success in the context of achieving your organization's dreams, especially a Big Dream or North Star vision. You are far less likely to become disappointed, discontent, and beat yourself up by assessing your achievements as a strategy leader by measuring backwards. Dreams and ideals serve to provide needed direction and inspiration, but they are not the best way to measure personal achievements.

You are encouraged to adopt this practice. And when you think about it, it is relevant to all people whether they are in a position of leadership or not. And it relevant to you beyond your leadership role, whether if be assessing your success in raising a family or improving your golf game.

And one last thought pertaining to the origin of the concept introduced here. Odds are that, given where you are and the fact and and the fact that you are reading this book, you are also a high achiever. But whether you are or not is not the point. The concept just makes a lot of sense.

CONCLUSION

The purpose of this book is to equip you, as a leader who wants to make a difference, with the requisite concepts, structures, practices, and tools to formulate and execute a sound strategy for your organization to move forward. Whether that be the organization as a whole or an organization unit.

Using the Strategic Framework model as the focus, the book is formatted to guide you through applying the complete planning cycle depicted by the model. Strategy formulation consisting of the identify and direction dimensions. And strategy execution which is working the strategy dimension.

I sincerely hope you found, and will continue to find, this book to be a valuable resource for you. Thinking and behaving strategically is not easy work. In fact, it is damn hard work. But oh, it is so vital if the organization is to experience true success, and to sustain such success. And, as cited in the book, research tells us that formulating and executing a sound strategy is the one area leaders struggle with the most. A large part of the reason is that most leaders so not know how to effectively go about it. Hopefully, this book fills that void for you. Now, go ahead and apply the necessary quality thinking and interacting to use the model to develop and implement a sound strategy for your organization.

All the best to you.

APPENDICES

OVERVIEW

....

Four of the structures included in these Appendices serve as valuable tools for you as a leader when collaborating with others, such as your leadership team, on important matters. These tools are especially valuable for facilitating quality thinking and interacting in formulating and executing strategy. The fifth structure is a personal development guide. *Self-Coaching,* Appendix E, included to help you work on any behavioral changes that you may want to work on.

The four collaboration tools were demonstrated or referenced at some point in the book.

The *Affinity Diagram*, Appendix A, is a powerful technique for generating and grouping large amounts of inputs in a creative and inclusive manner. It was demonstrated in chapter 2, *Clarifying Core Values*, as a way to obtain individual team member inputs, and then to convert such inputs to a consensus.

The *Gradients of Agreement Scale*, Appendix B, is an effective way to poll individual team members to determine the degree of support for a particular initiative before implementing it. This tool was referenced in chapter 2, *Clarifying Core Values*, as a way to get a specific idea of each individual team members support for the core values and their operating definitions before implementation.

The *Interrelationship Digraph*, Appendix C, is used to facilitate a logical sequence of activities toward a common end when such a sequence may not be obvious. This tool was demonstrated in chapter 8, *Charting a Strategic Path*, to illustrate how to sequence strategies listed in a strategic path to properly map out a master plan.

The *Goal Analysis* technique, Appendix D, is a tool whose process largely parallels that of the Affinity Diagram. The key distinction is the starting point. Whereas the Affinity Diagram is used to gather and sort a large number of inputs around a common theme; Goal Analysis starts with a specific goal or objective and is used to specify the conditions or evidences that exist when the objective is achieved. It answers the question: "What does success look like"?

Goal Analysis was referenced in chapter 9, *Planning Actions*, as an effective and comprehensive way of describing what success would look like if an objective for a specific action plan was achieved.

You are encouraged to use these tools to fully engage people as appropriate when working on important opportunities or challenges. They facilitate inclusive participation in achieving productive outcomes in an effective and efficient manner. Have fun using them and reaping the benefits. And make modifications as you see fit.

APPENDIX A

AFFINITY DIAGRAM*

What it is

The Affinity Diagram is a powerful technique for generating and grouping large amounts of information in a creative and consensual manner. The advantages of the technique include: (1) creatively generating information pertinent to the opportunity or challenge; (2) managing a large and possibly diverse and complex amount of information; and, (3) obtaining understanding, consensus, and commitment by all involved in the process.

The affinity diagram is far superior to the traditional "popcorn" type of brainstorming in that some discipline is inserted into the process and everyone is heard from. In traditional brainstorming the vocal participants often dominate and the quieter types, who may have a lot to offer, do not participate as much as they should. You will also find that you can get a lot done in a short time in using this tool.

When to Use

- To develop success criteria, desired outcomes, or decision criteria.
- To generate alternatives or options.
- To generate a list of possible opportunities or challenges.
- For developing various strategic planning statements such as core values or vision elements.

---

* Michael Bassard, *The Memory Jogger Plus+* (Methuen, MA, GOAL/QPC, 1989).

How to Use

Best used in groups up to 10 people. Subdivide into smaller groups of four to 10 if working with a larger group. After the subgroups have completed their work, the subgroups can discuss and consolidate their work to develop a single product. Assigning this task to representatives from each subgroup often works best in consolidating the small group products into a single product. The subgroup can report back to the larger group at a later date with their consolidation.

The Steps

1. Agree on the objective.

2. Have each member of the group silently write down her or his ideas on 3'x5" Post-It™ notes. One idea per note. Supply participants with black felt-tip pens. (Sharpie pens are great) to enhance readability. Each statement should be no more than a few words, and contain a verb and a noun to minimize ambiguity

3. After everyone has had a chance to complete their silent brainstorming, have them randomly post their notes to flip chart paper taped to a wall or laid out on a table. The sheets of paper allow you to Scotch Brand™ tape the eventual clusters of 3M Post-It™ notes for ease of transport and eventual typing.

   Discussion at this point is limited to questions of clarification that participants may have as they scan the posted notes. Participants are encouraged to add new ideas that may be triggered by the display of group ideas.

4. In silence, participants work on grouping and regrouping similar ideas. Allow everyone a chance to participate. Best to limit active involvement, that is, moving notes around, to

136

a maximum of five people at a time. Participants can trade off. Duplications can be discarded, but only if they are exact duplications. If an idea seems to belong in more than one cluster, duplicate the note. If a note does not logically into a cluster post it off to the side as an "outlier". Clusters will typically range from four to six.

5. Once the clusters are determined, discussion is allowed. Minor additional rearranging may occur at this time as participants clarify their understanding of what has been accomplished.

6. Once the clusters are clear and agreed upon, a header label is identified for each cluster. The header can be one of the cluster notes if it adequately summarizes the cluster information. If not, make up a header that does. The header must be specific and concise, a word or few words at the most, and still capture the meaning of the cluster. Draw a boundary around the header using a color other than black to distinguish it from the cluster notes and place it at the top of the cluster.

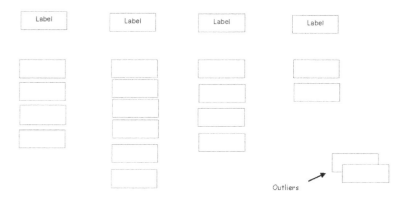

137

7. Expand each header into a sentence that captures the essence of that particular cluster.

Due to time considerations and to allow for adequate quality thinking and interacting, it is often advantageous to assign the task of expanding the headers into full sentences to an individual or subgroup who will report back to the full group at a later time.

APPENDIX B

GRADIENTS OF AGREEMENT SCALE*

Testing for Agreement

As a team leader you are naturally concerned as to what team members are thinking or feeling regarding key issues being discussed or decided.

Methods for testing for agreement are outlined below. The importance of the decision and its acceptance should dictate which consensus testing method is most appropriate.

Figure B.1 Testing for Agreement

Speculate	Speculate that it seems that consensus has been reached. Observe the reaction to the statement. Invite feedback.
Individual Polling	Ask each team member if she or he can support the decision being proposed.
Gradients of Agreement Scale	Poll the team using the Gradients of Agreement methodology described below.

The Gradients of Agreement Scale is an extremely effective way to poll the team to determine the degree of support for a proposed important decision before it is implemented.

* Sam Kaner with Lenny Lind, Catherine Toldi, Sarah Fisk, and Diane Berger, *Facilitator's Guide to Participatory Decision-Making* (Philadelphia, PA., New Society Publishers, 1996.)

The Gradients of Agreement Scale allows you as the leader to specifically assess the degree of support that exists for implementing the decision. If adequate support exists, you can feel confident that the decision will be effectively implemented. If adequate support for the decision does not exist, the process allows you and the team to identify specific implementation concerns and barriers. Given such input the you can assess if the decision needs to be reframed, or if implementation strategies need to be revised. Or whether the decision should be postponed or scrapped.

How to Use

1. Clearly state the proposal or decision.

2. Use the scale shown below to poll each team member. Change the wording if you wish. Replicate the scale on a flipchart or white board.

Gradients of Agreement Scale

The scale is a way to get beyond simple "yes" or "no" statements of support such as the individual polling method described above. "Yes" and "no" can have many different meanings. Using the scale makes it easier for group members to be honest and specific about their thoughts and feelings regarding the proposed decision. In addition, members can register less-than-whole-hearted support without fearing that their statement will be interpreted as a veto.

3. Decide how to take the poll.

    Options:

    *   Each individual gives rating and says why. No discussion.
    *   Show of hands working down the scale.
    *   Simultaneous declaration. Write down number and hold up.
    *   Secret ballot.

    The first option combined with a second round makes for an especially effective process in that individuals may want to change their voting after hearing others rationale on how why they voted the way they did.

4. Record the results on the flipchart or white board prepared in step 2.

For example:

1	2	3	4	5
Endorse	Agree, with reservations	Mixed thoughts and/ or feelings	Don't like... But won't block	Can't support
x	x	x	x	
x	x	x		
x	x			
x	x			
	x			

5. Determine if you are comfortable with the outcome to assure effective execution of the decision. If not, you may want to reframe the proposal or decision, revise implementation strategies, or postpone or scrap the decision.

APPENDIX C

INTERRELATIONSHIP DIGRAPH*

What It Is

A planning tool that takes a specific opportunity or challenge and maps out the logical sequential links amongst the contributing factors to the opportunity or challenge. The resulting diagram shows cause-and-effect relationships amongst the contributing factors. The main purpose of the diagram is to identify relationships that may not be easily recognizable.

When to Use

When working to logically sequence various factors impacting a specific opportunity or challenge when the relationship amongst the various factors may not be obvious. The sequence identified allows for the development of a logical course of action.

How to Use

1. Clearly define the opportunity or challenge.

2. Identify the key factors contributing to the opportunity or challenge.

3. Summarize each opportunity or challenge on a 3"x5" 3M Post-It™ note.

---

* Michael Bassard, *The Memory Jogger Plus+* (Methuen, MA, GOAL/QPC, 1989).

142

4. Arrange the Post-It™ notes in a circle or oval on a sheet of flip chart paper.

5. Determine the relationship between each of the factors by working clockwise around the circle or oval, taking one factor at a time and relating it to each of the other factors. In so doing, ask the questions for each paired comparison: a) "Does a relationship between these two factors exist?" b) "If a relationship does exist, which factor is the precursor of the other. In other words, which is the Driver (D), and which is the Result (R)?"

    Draw arrows between each paired comparison that has a relationship. Draw an arrow from the factor you are focusing on to each of the other factors it may influence or contribute to. In other words, serve as a precursor to that factor. Conversely, draw an arrow into the factor you are focusing on from any of the other factors that may serve as a precursor to it.

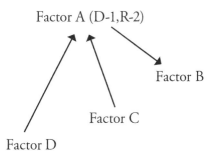

6. Tally the relationship arrows between each of the paired comparisons and show the tally next to the factor you are focusing on, as shown in the chart above.

7. Review your chart and determine the logical sequence.

Be aware that the number of arrows is only an indicator and not an absolute rule. Check to be sure that factors with fewer Ds should be moved up in your sequence.

An Example

From a leadership team that had identified five strategic imperatives n its strategic path to move them toward their vision of establishing a first-rate tennis operation for their country club. Each of the strategies is summarized in the form of a label.

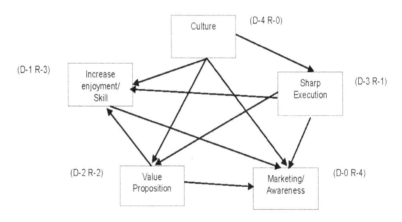

Sequence for Master Plan
1. Culture
2. Sharp Execution
3. Value Proposition
4. Increase Enjoyment/Skill
5. Marketing/Awareness

APPENDIX D

GOAL ANALYSIS*

....

What It Is

The Goal Analysis technique is a practical and proven procedure for sparking quality thinking to define success, for example, desired project outcomes or decision criteria. It allows you to go from a high order of abstraction to something concrete. It allows you to go from abstract language to specific language when needed to answer the question: "How do you know success when you see it"? "What are the specific evidences of success"?

The tool can be used you as an individual or when working with a group such as a leadership or planning team.

When to Use

When you need to translate abstract language (*"fuzzies"*) into specific or concrete terms before you can effectively proceed.

For example, an objective "to improve the safety consciousness of division operation and maintenance employees" leaves a lot of room for interpretation. What you would want to do is ask: *"How do you know good safety consciousness when you see it?"* That is, what is the target group doing when they are behaving in a "safety conscious" manner? Once you know the answer to this question in specific,

---

* Robert F. Mager, *Goal Analysis; How You Can Clarify Your Goals So You Can Actually Achieve Them* (CFP Press. 3rd Edition, 1979).

behavioral terms you can more effectively and efficiently proceed with your decision making.

The goal analysis technique is as an excellent tool to craft desired outcomes for a project objective when defining project specifications.

How to Use

1. Write down the **GOAL or OBJECTIVE.** A *goal* typically refers to a longer-range aspiration; whereas an *objective* typically refers to a shorter-term aspiration. There could be several objectives called for to achieve a specific goal or strategic imperative.

2. **JOT** down in words and phrases the evidences that, if achieved, would cause you to say that the goal was successful met.

3. **SORT** out the jottings into logical categories or clusters.

4. **LABEL** each cluster. Develop a "header" (just a word or two) for each cluster that summarizes the cluster

5. **EXPAND** each label into a statement that captures the essence of the ideas expressed in the cluster, that is, the jottings. Mentally preface each statement with the word "when", in that the statements represent the conditions that exist *when* the goal (objective) is achieved.

6. **TEST** the list of criteria. "If all of these criteria were being met, would I say the goal was being successfully met?" If the answer is "no", determine what is missing. If the answer is "yes", your goal analysis is complete.

APPENDIX E

SELF-COACHING

As we are all so well aware of, making behavioral change is often not all that easy. The guide below is a practical and proven way to help you think through what you may need to do and how to go about doing it in to make a behavioral change you wish to make.

The process:

1. Specifically *summarize the commitment* you want to make in a well-worded sentence.

2. How committed are you to making this change?

3. What have you *been doing/not been doing instead*?

4. *Why do you want to make this change?* Why is it important? What would happen if you did nothing?

5. What would success look like if you made this change?

   Use the Goal Analysis technique described in Appendix D to help you describe your desired outcomes.

6. Are there *any hidden competing commitments* that may be inhibiting you from making the desired change? For example, you may want to be a more collaborative leader, but your current mental models is that to do so would be perceived as a sign of weakness.

- What are the origins of any such competing commitments?

- What can you do to eliminate or minimize the impact of such competing commitments on making the change you want to make?

7. Could you make this change if you really wanted to?

- Do you have the *ability* to make the desired change? That is, could you do it if you really wanted to? If not, it may be something you just need to make the best of.

- If you think you have the ability to make the desired change, do you think you currently have the *knowledge* or *skill* necessary to make the change? If not, what are you lacking?

- What *resources* might you draw upon (for example, books, training courses or materials, people you respect and trust, and so forth) to help you gain the knowledge or skill you think you need?

In making personal behavioral changes, most often it is not a matter of not possessing the necessary skills, knowledge, or skill to make the change, the "can-dos". But rather, it is the commitment to make the desired change, the "will-do".

If you do have the ability to make the change, whether or not you need to acquire some additional knowledge or skill to make the change, it all comes down to your willingness to engage in the requisite behavior to make the desired change.

The steps below represent a practical and proven way for to go about making any personal behavioral changes you may want to make.

8. Identify *deliberate practices* to help you to make the desired behavioral change.

   Deliberate Practices are recurring behaviors you commit to engage in with a specific desired outcomes or standards in mind.

   For example, if you were serious about improving your golf game, you might commit to going to the golf range to practice on a regular basis. But in so doing, if you are really serious, you need to commit to working on specific aspects of your game with specific results in mind, that is deliberate practice. Rather than just banging the ball around or seeing how far you could hit it.

   What deliberate practices can you think of and are willing to engage in to help you make your desired change?

9. Identify *self-observation* questions to assess your progress.

   In many, if not most, of the desired personal behavioral changes one wants to make there are not convenient mechanisms to assess progress, such as driving ranges to assess your golfing progress, or scales to check your weight with regard to your diet program commitment. Self-observation questions are used instead.

   For example, in wanting to genuinely involve people more in staff meetings, a leader might ask him or herself at the conclusion of each staff meeting: "What did I do or not do to help or hinder staff participation in this meeting"? Such a self-observation question might be linked with a deliberate practice the leader previously committed to in connection with this commitment.

What self-observation questions should you ask yourself on a regular or defined basis to assess your progress in making your desired personal behavioral change?

10. *Measure backwards.*

Assessing personal achievement progress is best measured by looking back at what you have achieved to date on your journey, rather than looking forward at how far you have yet to go. You want to identify and celebrate the gains you have made rather than get frustrated and possibly give up by focusing on the gaps that exist between where you are and achieving your personal ideals.

You can discontinue consciously working on your desired personal behavioral change when you can truthfully say that it is a part of you now. In other words, it is now a part of your motor memory. Just like the grooved golf swing you developed that you keep honed but no longer have to think so much about it.

Sources that were useful in constructing this guide were:

Robert Kegan and Lisa Laskow Lahey, *Immunity to Change, How to Overcome It and Unlock the Potential in Yourself and Your Organization*, Harvard Business Pess, 2009.

Carl Welte, *Building Commitment: A Leader's Guide to Unleashing the Human Potential at Work,* Balboa Press, 2016.

Robert F. Mager, *Goal Analysis: How to Clarify Your Goals So You Really Can Achieve Them*, Third Edition, Center for Effective Performance, 1997.

James Flaherty, *Coaching: Evoking Excellence in Others,* Butterworth Heinemann, 1999.

Dan Sullivan and Dr. Benjamin Hardy, *The Gap and the Gain: The High Achievers' Guide to Happiness, Confidence, and Success*, Hay House, 2021.

ENDNOTES

Introduction
1. Carl Welte, *Building Commitment: A Leader's Guide to Unleashing the Human Potential at Work*, Balboa Press, 2016.

Chapter One
1. James Kouzes and Barry Posner, *The Leadership Challenge: How to Make Extraordinary Things Happen in Organizations,* 6th Edition, Jossey-Bass, 2017.
2. Ibid.
3. James C. Collins and Jerry Porras, *Built to Last: Successful Habits of Visionary Companies*, Harper Business, 1994.
4. Noel Tichy and Eli Cohen, *The Leadership Engine: How Winning Companies Build Leaders at Every Level*, Harper Business, 1997.

Chapter Two
1. Peter Drucker, *Management Tasks, Responsibilities, Practices,* Harper & Row Publishers, 1974.
2. Ibid.
3. Charles Handy, *The Age of Paradox*, Harvard Business School, 1994.
4. Peter Drucker, *The Essential Drucker*, Collins, 2001.

Chapter Three
1. James Kouzes and Barry Posner, *The Leadership Challenge: How to Make Extraordinary Things Happen in Organizations,* 6th Edition, Jossey-Bass, 2017.
2. Patrick Lencioni, *The Advantage: Why Organizational Health Trumps Everything Else in Business*, Jossey-Bass, 2012.
3. Ibid.
4. Terry Pearce, *Leading Out Loud: A Guide for Engaging Others in Creating the Future*, 3rd Edition, Jossey-Bass, 2013.
5. Ron Crossland, *Voice Lessons: Applying Science in the Art of Leadership Communication*, Ron Crossland, 2012.

6. Chip Heath and Dan Heath, *Make It Stick: Why Some Ideas Survive and Others Do Not*, Random House, 2007.

Chapter Four
1. Raymond E. Miles and Charles C. Snow, *Fit, Failure, and the Hall of Fame: How Companies Succeed or Fail*, The Free Press, 1994.
2. Guerillermo Marmol Jr., Michael Murray, Andreas Zielke, and Joseph A. Avila, eds., *The McKinsey Quarterly Anthologies: Growth Strategies: Planning, Genius, or Luck?,* McKinsey & Co., 1994.

Chapter Five
1. For a detailed discussion of the importance of WHY? See: Simon Sinek: *Start with WHY: How Great Leaders Inspire Everyone to Take Action*, Portfolio/Penguin, 2009.

Chapter Six
1. J. Allan McCarthy, *The Transition Equation: A Proven Strategy for Organizational Change*, Lexiington Books, 1996.
2. J. Allan McCarthy, *Beyond Genius, Innovation, & Luck: The Rocket Science of Building High-Performance Corporations* 4th Edition Publishing, 2011.

Chapter Seven
1. J. Allan McCarthy, *The Transition Equation: A Proven Strategy for Organizational Change*, Lexiington Books, 1996.
2. Adapted from: David J. Collins and Michael G. Rukstad, "Can You Say What Your Strategy Is?", *Harvard Business Review*, April 2008.

Chapter Eight
1. J. Allan McCarthy, *The Transition Equation: A Proven Strategy for Organizational Change*, Lexiington Books, 1996.
2. The need for reinventing strategy is backed by solid research, including that of Keith McFarland. In addition to studying nine breakthrough companies in detail, his research includes working in the field with fifty-two other companies over a five-year period across four continents. There was personal contact with 1, 441 Executives and managers. Keith R. McFarland, *The Breakthrough Company: How Everyday Companies Become Extraordinary Performers*, Three River Press, 2008.
3. McCarthy, op.cit.

Chapter Nine

1. Ray Dalio, *Principles*, Simon & Schuster, 2017.
2. J. Allan McCarthy, *Beyond Genius, Innovation, & Luck: The Rocket Science of Building High-Performance Corporations* 4th Edition Publishing, 2011.
3. Dalio, op.cit.

Chapter Ten

1. Terry Pearce, *Leading Out Loud: A Guide for Engaging Others in Creating the Future*, 3rd Edition, Jossey-Bass, 2013.
2. Ron Crossland, *Voice Lessons: Applying Science in the Art of Leadership Communication*, Ron Crossland, 2012.
3. Ibid.
4. Chip Heath and Dan Heath, *Make It Stick: Why Some Ideas Survive and Others Do Not*, Random House, 2007.
5. James Kouzes and Barry Posner, *Credibility: How Leaders Gain and Lose It, Why People Demand it*, Jossey-Bass, 1993.
6. Ibid.
7. Jim Collings, *Good to Great: Why Some Companies Make the Leap…and Others Don't*, Harper-Collins Publishing Company, 2001.
8. Berne Brown, *Dare to Lead: Brave Work. Tough Conversations. Whole Hearts.*, Random House, 2013.
9. Richard Bandler and John Grinder, *The Structure of Magic II: A Book about Communications and Change*, Prometheus Nemisis Books, 1978.
10. There are many providers of the DISC model and related assessments. If you are interested in learning more about DISC, I recommend Assessments 24x7. Their website is Assessments24x7.com. Also, Brandon Parker, Jennifer Larsen, and Tony Alessandra, *What Makes Humans Tick: Exploring the Best Validated Assessments*, Indie Books International, 2021.
11. Patrick Lencioni, *Death by Meeting: About Solving the Most Painful Problem In Business*, Jossey-Bass, 2004.
12. Ibid.
13. Ibid.
14. Simon Sinek, *The Infinite Game*, Portfolio/Penguin, 2019.
15. J. Allan McCarthy, *Beyond Genius, Innovation, and Luck: The Rocket Science of Building High-Performance Corporations*, 4th Edition Publishing, 2011.
16. James Kouzes and Barry Posner, *Encouraging the Heart: A Leader's Guide to Rewarding and Recognizing Others*, Jossey-Bass, 1999.

17. Robert Kaplan and David P. Norton, *The Balanced Scorecard: Translating Strategy into Action*, Harvard Business School Press, 1996.
18. Dan Sullivan and Dr. Benjamin Hardy, *The Gap and The Gain: The High Achievers' Guide to Happiness, Confidence, and Success*, Hay House Inc., 2021.

ABOUT THE AUTHOR

Carl Welte founded Welte Associates in 1993. Welte Associates enables organizational leaders and teams to achieve desired business results by helping them build the organizational capabilities to do so. That is, the requisite strategy, structure, systems, and workforce capability to succeed.

His many years of organizational, management, and consulting experience has equipped him with the requisite wisdom, consulting, and coaching skills to enable leaders and teams to effectively address their organization's opportunities and challenges.

He has held senior-level positions in both large and small organizations. Carl has also held leadership positions in a variety of professional, industrial, and educational associations.

Carl was a visiting faculty member for 12 years at the University of Idaho, teaching in its executive development program. He has also taught leadership and management programs in the University of California's extension learning system for more than 10 years.

His other books include *Building Commitment: A Leader's Guide to Unleashing the Human Potential at Work*, Balboa Press, 2016, and *Communicating about Differences: Understanding, Appreciating and Talking about Divergent Points of View*, Balboa Press, 2021.

He has an MBA from the University of California, Berkeley, and a BS degree in business administration from the University of California.

Carl lives in Novato, CA with his wife Dee. They have three children, six grandchildren, and one great grandchild.

He can be reached at:

Welte Associates
14 Plata Court
Novato, CA 94947
Phone: (415) 328-1349
Email: carl@welte.com
Website: welte.com

CPSIA information can be obtained
at www.ICGtesting.com
Printed in the USA
BVHW031354140322
631401BV00001BA/61

9 781957 203188